THE OTHER TRADITION

OF MODERN

ARCHITECTURE

THE UNCOMPLETED PROJECT

Colin St John Wilson

black dog
publishing

THE OTHER TRADITION
OF   MODERN
ARCHITECTURE

THE UNCOMPLETED PROJECT

Colin St John Wilson

FOREWORD

ELLIS WOODMAN

Sifting through the history of architecture one encounters successive polemical texts that have impacted on the imaginations of practitioners with a frankly inexplicable force. Certainly, it is hard to think of which other artistic discipline has proved quite so susceptible to the promptings of the written word. Where in the history of painting or of cinema, or of opera is the manifesto that has exerted the influence that could be claimed for, say, Le Corbusier's *Vers une Architecture*? The phenomenon is all the more curious in that so many of the key texts of architectural theory are the work of young architects who had yet to build on any scale. One can be sure that the profession would have tracked a very different path over the past century were it not for the shepherding of such relative innocents as Adolf Loos, Le Corbusier, Aldo Rossi, Robert Venturi and Denise Scott Brown and Rem Koolhaas.

As a treatise penned by an architect with decades of practice behind him *The Other Tradition* is therefore something of a rarity. You will find, I think, that this proves a significant distinction. Unlike so many architectural manifestos this book doesn't set out an abstract ideology against which practitioners might model their work. Indeed its argument is an indictment of exactly such doctrinaire thinking. For Colin St John Wilson the value of a building lies not in its correspondence to a pre-established ideal but in the artfulness with which it accommodates practical contingencies. His book is, in short, a call for an understanding of architecture as a practical art.

Or, I should say: a return to such an understanding. As the author establishes, it was only with the ascendancy of the Ecole des Beaux Arts that art and functionality came to be seen as divergent and even opposing architectural values. It was a false polarity that, for all their functionalist rhetoric, many in the Modern Movement proved only too ready to adopt. Many but not all. The book's title refers to a wide constellation of talent that Wilson persuasively corrals into a marginal but persistent counter-tendency — a resistance movement opposed to modernism's reduction to a formulaic schema, unresponsive to the vagaries of human life.

In its early years, Wilson's Other Tradition was dominated by architects who communicated their position almost exclusively through building. Figures like Alvar Aalto and Hans Scharoun couldn't compete with

Le Corbusier's powers on the soapbox and showed little inclination to do so. In a sense, *The Other Tradition*, is the manifesto that these laconic masters never wrote. As such, it enjoys one considerable advantage over the texts that did emerge at the time from the CIAM-endorsed mainstream — namely, over half a century of hindsight. Wilson mercilessly documents how the passage of time has revealed canonical works by Le Corbusier, Walter Gropius and Ludwig Mies van der Rohe to be the products of a near-tyrannical mindset. In each case he builds up a damning case that an adherence to architectural dogma was privileged over an accommodation of the most basic human needs. By comparison, the buildings that Wilson posits as the founding works of the Other Tradition speak with undiminished eloquence. Their enduring functionality has ensured that they remain well loved and artistically alive.

It is a little over a decade since this book was first published and one suspects that it will be read rather differently now from how it was then. In 1994, it could be taken as a rebuke to the then still prevalent forces of historical revisionism. Over the proceeding 20 years, the legacy of Modernism had fallen under a sustained assault from a loose affiliation of postmodernists, neo-traditionalists, sociologists, heritage lobbyists and community groups. The attack was nowhere more forcefully delivered than in Britain where, in his role as architect of the British Library, Wilson had come under fire from the figurehead of the anti-modernist faction — the Prince of Wales. Historical subtleties were an early casualty of this bun-fight and the Modern Movement was all too quickly caricatured as a monolithic phenomenon, uniformly ahistorical in mindset and avowedly committed to values of wholesale reinvention and brute standardisation. In this context, *The Other Tradition* made a powerful case that, in so far as it was a movement at all, modernism was always a far more multi-faceted one than its opponents would have us believe.

12 years on, one could conclude that the fight for the future of modernism has been won. The heat has gone out of both the postmodern and neo-traditional causes and architecture of a modern stripe enjoys an extraordinary level of acceptance from Edinburgh to Dubai. However, after reading *The Other Tradition* one might well ask: which modernism won? Looking through any of the innumerable architecture magazines

now in circulation, you would struggle to find much that spoke of the values of a figure like Aalto. Indeed you would find no shortage of buildings that posited so dislocated a relationship between form and function as to have been entirely unimaginable when *The Other Tradition* was first published.

The 'iconic building' has become the paradigm of the age — a building that suppresses social, contextual and even technical considerations in pursuit of a startling, immediately apprehensible image. The unique spectacle has become all and accordingly, it is the architects whose powers of formal reinvention are the most untiring, that are deemed our modern masters. The market rewards them with the opportunity to build on an unprecedented scale while reducing them to something perilously close to branding consultants. Endless novelty has become a doctrine every bit as unbending as Le Corbusier's Five Point Plan.

The irony of this situation is evident even to those who are most embroiled in it. "It is really unbelievable what the market demands [from architecture] now", bemoans Rem Koolhaas. "It demands recognition, it demands difference and it demands iconographic qualities." So prevalent have such values become in the West that our flying Dutchman is forced to search for commissions of a more believable nature in the most unlikely places: "Money is not the final arbiter in China, even though it has become here", he suggests. "[In China] there is still some lingering sympathy for programmatic issues, like how things work and how they have to perform."[1]

Thankfully, not all intelligent Western architects have felt the need to adopt quite such a drastic course of action. Figures such as Alvaro Siza and Raphael Moneo continue to make work in Europe that offers a vital alternative to the culture of endless spectacle. One can trace their influence in the work of a number of younger practices — many of them British. Here for example, is a statement of intent from Sergison Bates Architects:

> We resist the abstract ideology that reduces architecture to a product,
> imposing itself autonomously from its site and often even of its use.
> This method of production gives a generalising effect to the character
> of place and seeks credibility in being formally inventive and 'new'.[2]

The complaint is picked up by their contemporary Adam Caruso of Caruso St John:

> Mainstream practice has embraced the rhetoric of the market to make work that is infused with brand recognition. Strategies of cybernetics, phylogenics, parametrics, mapping — each strive to generate completely original forms, unusual shapes, in plan, in section sometimes both. These bold profiles can amplify or even replace corporate logos.... Architecture is now practised at an unprecedented global scale, and the major players seem to be egging each other on. Who will produce the largest, and most formally outlandish project? Who will finally say stop? Never has so much construction been based on so few ideas.[3]

Young architects such as those quoted are searching for values on which to base their practice. They are finding them not through recourse to brittle doctrines, but like Aalto and Scharoun before them, through close observation of the given conditions of a project — the qualities of a site, the requirements of a brief, the capacity of building materials to make characterful, responsive spaces. Our increasing awareness of the environmental consequences of building in a generalised and unsustainable manner lends that effort a new sense of urgency. In this harsh context, the publication of this new edition of *The Other Tradition* is particularly welcome. If modernism has a future one senses that it will necessarily develop from the work that Wilson celebrates in these pages.

NOTES—FOREWORD

1   "Koolhaas lambasts idolatry", *Building Design*, 20 February 2004.
2   *2G: Sergison Bates*, Barcelona: Gustavo Gilli, 2005.
3   *As built: Caruso St John Architects*, Madrid: A+T Ediciones, 2005.

PROLOGUE

COLIN ST JOHN WILSON

In a celebrated lecture at the Royal Institution in London in 1978, Giancarlo de Carlo recounted a number of "the promises that the Modern Movement did not keep"; and, as one of the most lucid critics within the Movement, his account was severe and still remains unanswered. However, he did also throw in the aside: "The Modern Movement has 'died' many times", as if to say there is still life in the old dog yet. It is the thesis of this book that the Movement did not die but rather that its authority was usurped, right at the moment of its emergence into public identity, at the foundation of the International Congress of Modern Architects. It is not so much that "the good intentions of modern architecture" were not fulfilled but rather that they were abandoned at birth.

This is not a question of easy hindsight. By the mid-1930s, as the policies of CIAM emerged in Congresses at Frankfurt, Brussels and Athens, and a formula for "The International Style" was canonised, lone voices of dissent were raised. Alvar Aalto (perhaps because he was the youngest of the "Masters of the Heroic Period") saw the enemy to be not the wicked Past but the "bad faith" of the Present and he challenged the received doctrine of Congress right from the start. By 1940, he wrote of "the first and now past, phase of modern architecture" and argued that "it was not the rationalisation that was wrong but the fact that the rationalisation has not gone deep enough.... The newest phase of architecture tries to project rational methods from the technical field out to human and psychological fields."[1] What he meant in terms of architectural politics is made clear by his later statement about the revolution of Modern architecture that "like all revolutions, begins with enthusiasm and ends in some form of Dictatorship".[2]

This book begins with the argument that the Dictatorship set in at the very first meeting of CIAM at La Sarraz in June 1928. The plot is announced like a courtroom scene in a theatre. At that meeting, an orthodoxy and its priesthood were established with something of the fervour (not to forget ruthlessness) of the political seizures of power upon which it was, in part, modelled. Indeed, it is very disturbing to read in retrospect the extent to which Le Corbusier, who dedicated his city-planning proposals of the time to "Authority", quite frankly professed that these proposals would have to be imposed by a ruling caste; and he was prepared to go to any length in pursuit of the power to put his ideas into practice in the teeth of all opposition. The 'Open Hand' was always ready to become a closed fist.[3]

But unlike the political 'putsch', assent on matters of doctrine was not won without dispute. Hugo Haering, who was the leader of the German group of architects, lodged a protest in the cause of an architecture that would not impose a regime of pre-ordained geometrical forms on the one hand, nor the mass-produced models of industrial technology on the other. His plea for a less impatient, less pre-judged enquiry into the way things "wanted to be" was brushed aside in favour of an activism that, at one end of the scale, promoted the evolution of an *Existenzminimum*, and at the other, a city divided into "Four Functions". The victorious Establishment (the spokesman of which was Le Corbusier, and the cleric Giedion) anathematised and expelled the heretic. So much has eventually crept into the standard histories of the time.

What has not been so commonly recognised is that, at that moment, a sort of 'Resistance' was born — not a Resistance Movement (for there was no organised structure like the established Congress) but a widely dispersed constellation of architects in whose work the original intentions of that Movement lived on unabated. Pre-eminent among these was Alvar Aalto, whose RIBA discourse in 1957 was, for the present author, a profound revelation and the inspiration for a critical stance maintained and developed ever since. He spoke then of:

> the one good thing that we still have today — architects with a new approach [who] from being formal artists have moved over into a new field and they are the 'garde d'honneur', the hard-fighting squadron for the humanising of technology in our time.[4]

Nearly 40 years later, I believe that the buildings and theory of these architects reveal an alternative philosophy that is something much broader than the protest of eccentric individuals and now begins, on the evidence of 70 years work, to have the authority of an Other Tradition.

Insofar as it is a critique of the orthodox Modern Movement, it has two unique qualities. Firstly, it was generated within that movement rather than mounted from outside in the ranks of those who, in the current convention, saw the dispute in terms of "Ancient versus Modern". It is, therefore, creative and offers alternative models rather than disbelief and aggression. Second, those models were not hypothetical but took the form of actual buildings. They are buildings that have enjoyed satisfied occupation for 50 to 60 years, the proof of which rests in their excellent preservation. We are thus offered the ideal opportunity to judge by living evidence the efficacy of the alternative proposition.

The second part of the book explores the theoretical positions that lay behind 'what went wrong'. (There is a venerable saying that when fish go rotten they stink first in the head!) In trying to explain the nature of what Aalto called "les deux cochons — formalism and technology", it became clear that much of what was misconceived derived from a battle lost long before, in the eighteenth century. For the application to architecture of Kant's definition of aesthetics as the pursuit of 'the purposeless' drove a stake into the heart of architecture, splitting it into 'architecture' (fine art) and 'building' (utility). At one blow the concept which was fundamental to Classical Greek thought and which conceived of the beautiful and the purposeful as one thing (to *kalon*) was split into two elements which were then conceived to be in competition with each other. This particular blasphemy against classical values also did violence to another tenet which was equally fundamental to Greek culture — namely the distinction between a Fine Art "that served only itself, and a Practical Art" that served an end other than itself.

Both Bruno Zevi and John Summerson have drawn attention to what they consider to be the uniquely new element offered by the Modern Movement, namely a more methodical and answerable response to 'the Programme'; but to say that is simply to use another set of terms for what is meant by saying that architecture serves an end other than itself.[5] I put the point more strongly by saying that it is not so much a 'new' element produced by the Modern Movement as the revival of the most ancient mandate of all! The Greeks had no doubts about the matter. For them, architecture was clearly seen to belong to the category of Practical Art whose virtue lay in the Aristotelian "fulfilment of purpose".

And so, unexpectedly, I found that it was necessary to my argument to bring back to life two terms that have lost their true meaning in our time — 'the Classical' and 'the Functional'. The Classical has been robbed of all connection to its roots in ancient Greek thinking and rendered vacuous as a 'style' ('Postmodern') in a supposedly brave attempt to bring back 'enchantment' to a disillusioned public. The Functional has also been debased into its very opposite — once again a 'style' to prolong the old "Battle of the Styles" by the very people who should have protected its fundamental humanity.

The third part of the book is given to demonstration through case studies, using the comparative method, which throws into clear relief the differences between two alternative solutions to a common brief. In this exercise, I have deliberately chosen examples from the 1930s to the 1950s because on the one hand, I have been trying to track a 'heresy' down to its historical source, and on the other, I have tried to give substance to the claim of an 'Other Tradition' of the Modern Movement that has been pursued over a period of 70 years.

This book is an attempt to bring into focus a thesis that first emerged in a tentative fashion in my previous book *Architectural Reflections*.[6] That book addressed individually the buildings and ideas of certain architects and philosophers to whom I had been greatly attracted. When these, initially unrelated, findings were brought together, it became apparent that they shared an underlying common structure of intentions and advocacies. It is that common structure which I have tried to draw out here, rather than the unique properties of individual architects pursued for their own sake. As an archaeologist who puts together scattered fragments which gradually reveal a common foundation, so I have found a central theme that tied together what was most critical in the work of these architects. The further I have delved, the more convinced I have become; but in doing so, however, I have found that I was drawn to dig even deeper to follow the clues which led to some ancient and long-lost themes from the past. And so the use of the word 'other' in my title is intended to cover not only a school of thought in this century, but also to claim for that school authentic roots in classical Greek thought.

NOTES——PROLOGUE

1   Aalto, Alvar, "The Humanizing of Architecture" (1940), *Sketches*, first edition, MIT Press, Cambridge, MA: 1978.
2   Aalto, Alvar, "The Architectural Struggle", RIBA Discourse, London, 1957.
3   Fishman, Robert, "From the Radiant City to Vichy", *The Open Hand*, ed. Walden, MIT Press, Cambridge, MA: 1977. See also the texts in the syndicalist journal *Plans* that Le Corbusier edited from 1931–1932.
4   Aalto, "The Architectural Struggle".
5   Zevi, Bruno, *Towards an Organic Architecture*, London: Faber & Faber, 1941 and John Summerson, "The Case for a Theory of Architecture", *RIBA Journal*, June 1957.
6   St John Wilson, Colin, *Architectural Reflections*, Oxford: Butterworth Heinemann, 1992.

Copies of the original edition of this book were destroyed by the publishers to make way for space in their warehouse. However, word had got out and during the last ten years I have been flattered by letters of frustration both from the UK and from as far afield as Australia, South Africa and Cuba seeking copies. I was therefore very happy when Duncan McCorquodale of Black Dog Publishing offered to re-issue the book.

The message is even more urgent now than originally. The sideshow of Postmodern Neo-Classicism has faded from sight but it has been replaced by its opposite pole — a born-again Expressionism. (Such are the vagaries when fashion is the driving force!) When Frank Gehry discovered that computerised graphics enable you to do what architects were not able to do in 1918–1922, namely to build any shape whatsoever, then the game of sensational "Icons" became a world-wide gambit in the rivalry for cities in search of tourists. In itself, the ebullience is remarkable: the actual products, however, are above all remarkable for the brutal indifference of their impact upon the neighbourhood on which they have landed as if from the Moon: and the eye-catching irrationalism of their form is epitomised by a recent art gallery which does not appear to have a single vertical wall on which to hang a painting. Far from deepening the capacity of architecture to become a practical celebration of the joys of life, these phenomena have become sensational 'one-liners' that offer no resource for the kind of multi-layered engagement with the visitors that could keep the experience alive after the initial shock.

Mercifully, I sense that among the younger generation of architects there is a reaction similar to that of Nauman who, at the birth of the twentieth century, said "we have had enough of the extraordinary: what we need is the self-evident". A phrase that I often hear now is the pursuit of "the poeties of the ordinary". I hope that the re-issue of this book will help these architects to re-form the ranks of the avant-garde that gave birth to the original emancipatory commitment of the Modern Movement in its aim for the engagement and participation of 'the man-in-the-street'.

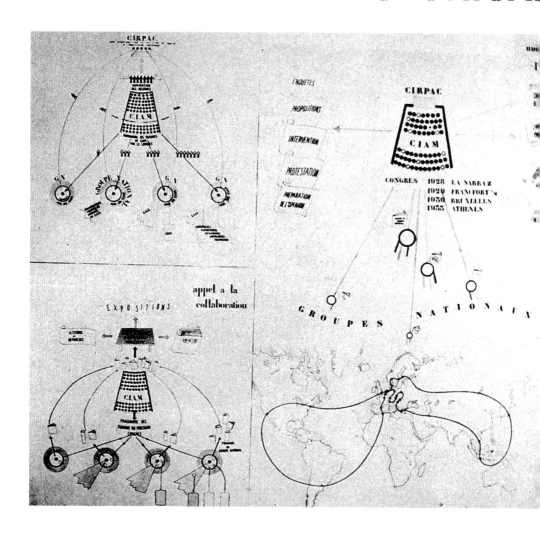

CONTEXT: WHAT WENT WRONG?

CHAPTER ONE

THE FIRST EPISODE
THE BATTLE OF LA SARRAZ

The architectural revolution, like all revolutions, begins with enthusiasm and ends in some form of Dictatorship.

ALVAR AALTO

Upon receiving the RIBA Gold Medal in 1957.

There has never been a moment in the history of architecture so rich in the variety of building forms and so violent in the polarity of ideological affirmations as that which prevailed ten years after the end of the First World War. A single publication presented a range of manifestos embracing the exuberance of Expressionism, the mystical fanaticism of De Stijl, the bracing coolness of *die Neue Sächlichkeit*, the wild invention of the Constructivists, the brooding complexity of the Organic School, and the Rationalism of the Purists.[1] The rival claims to orthodoxy were wide and contradictory but yet united in the generosity and optimism of their faith in the powers of architecture to make possible a change of heart. Yet within ten years that jolting energy and all that clamour in the forum had apparently been reduced to a single orthodoxy. How did this happen? The story is not as simple as it has been made to appear.

During the three previous years a number of events which had been given wide publicity interlocked in such a way as to suggest a sequence of transparent inevitability: Le Corbusier's *Pavillion de L'Esprit Nouveau* in the Paris Exposition of 1925; the *Competition for the Headquarters of the League of Nations* of 1926–1927; and the construction of the *Stuttgart Weissenhofsiedlung* Exhibition of 33 dwellings by 17 architects in 1927.[2] Parallel with this, a number of publications heralding the birth of a so-called 'International Architecture' appeared and so the expectation ran high for the formation of an established organisation that could promote this common cause through meetings, exhibitions and publications.[3]

Indeed, at the time of the Weissenhofsiedlung Exhibition itself, Hugo Haering, the secretary of the dominant group of architects in Berlin, called "Der Ring", had hoped to launch just such an international group out of the membership of the architects participating in that exhibition. However, following early disagreements over the initial layout of the exhibition with Mies van der Rohe (who had the overall role of master-planner) Haering had withdrawn from the scene and nobody else took up the proposal. What then happened has been described by Sigfried Giedion as follows:

In February 1928 I received a letter from Mme Hélène de Mandrot from La Sarraz saying that she would come to visit me in Zurich. When I met her at the station and before we left the platform, she began to disclose the purpose of her coming. She wanted to invite the outstanding contemporary architects of Europe to meet at her castle of La Sarraz, some miles north of Lake Geneva in the Canton de Vaud, Switzerland.

Mme de Mandrot had previously spoken with Le Corbusier and other friends in Paris. The time seemed ripe for all the protagonists of the different architectural developments in Austria, Belgium, France, Germany, Holland, Italy, Spain and Switzerland to come together in a neutral, central place in Europe....

In June 1928 the representatives of the different countries sat together in the Gothic chapel of the castle of La Sarraz discussing and building up what was later called the Manifesto of La Sarraz.... The association then formed was called the Congrès Internationaux d'Architecture Moderne — in abbreviated form, CIAM. The word 'congress' was used in its original sense of a 'marching together'.[4]

It is a significant fact that the architects participating in that first Congress not only represented eight countries but also a wide range in age difference and a yet wider range of the various avant-garde positions to which I have referred. Hendrik Petrus Berlage, Gerrit Rietveld and Mart Stam from Holland; Hugo Haering, Hannes Meyer and Ernst May from Germany; Karl Moser, Hans Schmidt, Rudolf Steiger and Max Ernst Haefeli from Switzerland; Alberto Sartoris and Carlo Enrico Rava from Italy; Victor Bourgeois from Belgium; Josef Frank from Austria; Le Corbusier, André Lurçat, Pierre Chareau and Gabriel Guevrekian from France; Fernando García Mercadal and Juan de Zavala from Spain. In spite of this diversity, however, the simple fact is that the thinking was dominated by Le Corbusier. He had been the first to be consulted by Mme de Mandrot, and he had drawn up the agenda and priorities for discussion in a *plan de bataille*. This took the form of six questions strictly limited to technology and not expecting to engage with questions of architectural aesthetic:

1. Modern technology and its consequences
2. Standardisation
3. Economy
4. Urbanism
5. Education
6. Realisation: Architecture and the state.[5]

He had virtually written the conclusions before the event.

The dominant thinking was grounded in three impulses. Politically it deployed the tactics and terminology of the revolutionary: there was to be a General Assembly with its delegates, committees and working-parties involved in active intervention, protest, re-shaping public opinion through publications and exhibitions and, inevitably, demanding conformity of idea in the interest of unity — "marching together". Philosophically it was cast in the mould of Descartes (the adjective 'Cartesian' explicitly and constantly used) whose method proposed the breaking down of all complex wholes into sub-problems of more manageable size, thereby eliminating contradictions and making possible simple formulae. Architecturally, it was to conform to the canonical "Five Points of Architecture" defined by Le Corbusier in 1926 as the intrinsic (and therefore inevitable!) language to be extrapolated from the new technical possibilities presented by steel and reinforced concrete. As demonstrated by Le Corbusier himself, that canon carried enormous authority by virtue of his poetic and concise gifts, but in the debate its status was strongly contested by Hannes Meyer, Ernst May and Gerrit Rietveld.

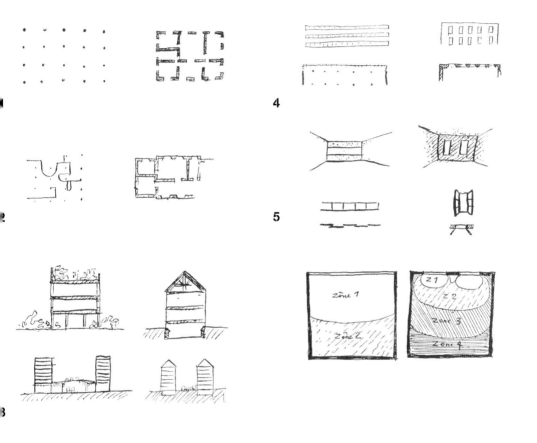

4

5

Le Corbusier
The Five Points of Architecture
1. Piloti: The house raised on loadbearing columns, — the garden beneath
2. The Free Plan
3. The garden on the roof
4. The window from side to side
5. The Free Facade.

It had been stipulated that one of the aims of the Congress was to "affirm a unity of viewpoint on the fundamental conceptions of architecture" and on that score too, some conflict of opinion was to be expected.[6] However, Le Corbusier was both persistent and persuasive; and agreement upon method was enough to smother substantial differences between his Cartesian Rationalism on the one hand and the *Neue Sächlichkeit* preoccupations of the German delegates. In particular it was enough to obtain assent from the hard-line 'Functionalists' — Meyer, Stam, Schmidt and Lurçat — whose shared commitment to the cause of Communism and to a solution to '*le problème du grand nombre*' led them to give priority to industrialised and standardised building: certainly they were being offered precisely the tool that they wanted — an instruction manual with clear directives for the fieldworkers.

But with Hugo Haering it was a different matter. He was an architect-philosopher of high reputation in Germany, a close friend of Hans Scharoun and Mies van der Rohe with whom he shared an office, fully armed with his own Functional theory of "new building". Returning to the scene after the failure of his attempt to launch just such a congress to coincide with the Stuttgart Exhibition, he disagreed with Le Corbusier both in fundamental values and the methods by which they were to be pursued. Even 20 years later he was to publish an article entitled "The World Is Not Yet Quite

Ready"; all the more so did he then challenge what he saw to be one
pre-judgement after another — ideal geometry, Cartesian method, the
Five Point canon and so on.7 He had already declared his opposition to
Le Corbusier in an article discriminating between architecture viewed as a
'Fine Art' and what he called "the new building" viewed as a 'Practical Art'.
He saw Le Corbusier as promoting the imposition of geometrical order
upon nature and upon the spontaneous and unpredictable manifestations
of human society. Indeed, the occasion for his protest could almost be
summarised in the opening of Descartes' *Discourse on Method*, which
seized upon the notion of the perfect city, "geometric and regular as an
architect's plan", as an analogue for Cartesian method:

> Laid out like the garden of Versailles in a rigid and geometric pattern,
> this town was to capture in a fixed network of parallel and radiating
> lines all of those confused and contrary organisms which the strange
> evolution of civic society had brought into being. Around the magic
> cross of coordinates the public monuments and private dwellings of this
> city, the shops and playhouses and factories, the schools and prisons
> and churches, were to dance eternal quadrilles with the precise elegance
> of lines and points in a theorem of Euclid. An irrational reality, a
> phenomenon biological in origin and in development, was thus to be
> made conformable to a pure creation of the mind.8

It is arguable that addiction to the Cartesian method is both the strength and the flaw in Le Corbusier's work. The procedure whereby a problem is broken down into distinct sub-problems has aesthetic advantages. In the first number of *L 'Esprit Nouveau* he wrote, "there is no work of art without system". This is clearly depicted in Charles Correa's demonstration of a sequence of analytical diagrams of the Mill Owner's building in Ahmedabad as a layering in depth of independent sub-systems of building components (structure, enclosure, sun-breaker), in which visual vitality springs from the juxtaposition of one element upon another.

On the other hand, when he writes that "the house must be disengaged once and for all from the street", he is writing a formula for the destruction of the city, and it is not long before the full horror of the city of 'Four Functions' is upon us. It is to the credit of his genius as an artist that the trauma of city planning in our time is in large part due to the Jekyll and Hyde talent of this brilliant and wrongheaded man whose gifts of persuasion were as powerful as his gift of invention.

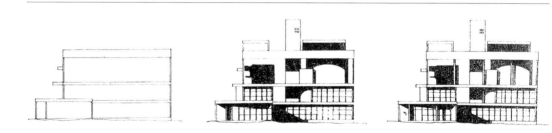

Charles Correa
Formal analysis of Le Corbusier's
Mill Owners' Building, Ahmedebad.
Decomposition of the Facade in accordance
with "the Five Points".

The core of Descartes' philosophy revolved around explanation in mechanistic terms. The analogy with the rational machine that colours all of his philosophy has dominated French thinking ever since and came easily to the lips of Le Corbusier, in whose view we live in a "machine-age civilisation", the eye being "*une machine admirable*", the work of art "*une machine à émouvoir*" and a home "*une machine à habiter*". As we shall see, this mechanistic explanation is deeply antipathetic to the Classical teleological account, which is based upon the fulfilment of purpose rather than elegance of performance.

To this concept of architecture as a pre-ordained language grounded in geometry and committed to imposing a timeless order upon the complexity of human society, Haering opposed a concept of "the new building" whose ancestry he claimed to lie in a tradition, older by far, of building organically in terms of the balance of nature, and man's responsibilities both to it and to his own desires — in short, to the things that have not changed. And in the present context of seeking solutions to

the problems of the day, he claimed that "we want to examine things and allow them to discover their own forms. It goes against the grain with us to bestow a form upon them from the outside, to determine them from without, to force upon them laws of any kind, to dictate to them."[9] Instead of Rationalism he sought an understanding of life's complexity; instead of order, participation. The term that he constantly uses is *Leistungsform*, which is the form that arises from performance or pattern of operations. Each task will, in his view, require its special order of performance to obtain fulfilment.

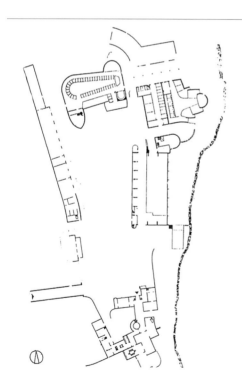

GUT GARKAU

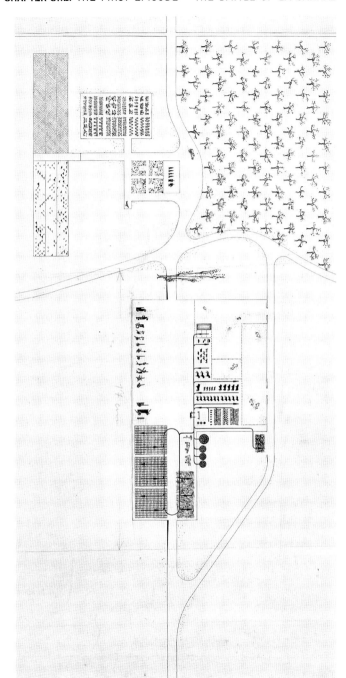

OPPOSITE
LEFT AND RIGHT:
Hugo Haering
Gut Garkau,
1922–1926.
Plan and axonometric
drawing.

RIGHT:
Le Corbusier
The Radiant Farm, 1938.
Plan FLC 20275.

One example of the differences in value that emerge from their two approaches is the different ways in which light is talked about. For Le Corbusier, light is the mechanism that delineates forms clearly as geometrical objects. For Haering (and, as we shall later see in our case studies, for both Eileen Gray and Alvar Aalto) it is the subtle, constantly changing medium that envelops and vivifies all our activities at all times and all seasons. Among Le Corbusier's Five Points, one of the by-products of the "free facade" is that it maximises the introduction of light from the external wall. For Haering, the qualities of light are a more complex matter:

> The best light for a room is light from above: toplight illuminates a room evenly and brings light from above as nature does. Light from the side is bad as it illuminates inadequately and creates too many shadows. It prevents a good and free placing of furniture, particularly desk, dining table, and washstand. Sidelighting admits the sun only for a short time: with toplights it lasts. A further advantage is that a toplit room is independent of orientation.[10]

The difference between his theoretical position and that of Le Corbusier is demonstrated quite transparently in the comparison between the farm he had built at Gut Garkau a few years earlier and Le Corbusier's later (unbuilt) project for the Radiant Farm.

TOP:
Hugo Haering
Gut Garkau,
1922-1926.

BOTTOM:
Le Corbusier
The Radiant Farm, 1938.
Plan FLC 28621.

We will return to this argument later when we explore the nature of the 'Other' order.[11] For the moment, however — the political moment — it was clear that Haering would lose the day. No revolutionary taskforce ever had time 'to examine things' and certainly never the wish 'to allow them to discover' anything of their own. Furthermore, there was considerable personal animosity between Haering and Le Corbusier (and his ally, the deeply committed Secretary of the Congress, Sigfried Giedion). It was deemed necessary for the delegates to close ranks, affirm solidarity, and write the Manifesto, "putting architecture back on its real plane — the economic and social plane".[12] The city was to be analytically broken down into "the organisation of the four functions of collective life — dwelling, work, recreation, transportation", for which "present technical means, which multiply ceaselessly, are the very key".[13] Finally, a programme of themes was to be devised for future meetings, and the first of these to be chosen for the next congress the following year in Frankfurt was the concept of the *Existenzminimum* for mass housing.

OPPOSITE
LEFT AND RIGHT:
Rudolf Schindler
How House,
Los Angeles, 1925.
Interior and exterior.

TOP AND BOTTOM:
Eileen Gray
Tempe à Pailla,
Castellar, 1932.
Interior and exterior.

RIGHT:
Le Corbusier
Letter to Giedion,
03.02.1929.

FAR RIGHT:
Johannes Duiker
Cineac,
Amsterdam, 1934.

With Haering duly silenced, there came into being, in June 1928, the established form for the future International Congresses of Modern Architecture (CIAM): protest had been dealt with and the new law had been laid down, albeit written in the language of the outlaw.

In that same year Hannes Meyer, the arch-Functionalist, was expelled from his post as Head of the Bauhaus. And with the rise to power of Hitler, the German Communists departed to Russia *en masse*: conformity in CIAM was virtually absolute and institutionalised on the basis of the resolutions passed in three Congresses — Frankfurt 1929, Brussels 1931 and Athens 1933. The one objector who had engaged in serious disagreement with Le Corbusier was now silenced by outright expulsion. Hugo Haering had now been superseded by Walter Gropius, who then chose Marcel Breuer as his supporting delegate rather than Haering — both of whom then vanished to the United States. In a letter to Giedion, Le Corbusier exulted in Haering's defeat with a cruel caricature of a herring with a priest's hat, a halo and an umbrella in full flight.

Expulsion may well be the way of dealing with dissent in terms of *realpolitik*, but it is no answer to the question that had been raised. Haering's expulsion was echoed in the withdrawal of other members of the Berlin Ring — Scharoun, Erich Mendelsohn and Bruno Taut. And it is as if, with his expulsion, a signal went out to that wider circle of ebullient and contending energies whose movements we have noted as the source of vitality of the early 1920s. As with the Bolsheviks, a small well-organised party had taken over the means of communication and set up a certain orthodoxy — in Alvar Aalto's phrase, the Revolution was well on its way to becoming "a Dictatorship". Indeed, it was not long before Le Corbusier, primed with his authoritarian syndicalist plan to change the whole world by means of architecture, was pleading his cause at the Court of Mussolini.[14]

I contend that at that moment a form of Resistance came into being. It was not a Resistance Movement with either the intention (or the organisation) to challenge that of CIAM but a number of independent practitioners, all of whom were ostensibly members of the Modern Movement but who professed to a wider and deeper point of view.

A few, like Aalto, still occasionally attended the CIAM meetings but more often than not — as in the case of the proposal to authorise a minimal dwelling unit (the *Existenzminimum* theme at Frankfurt) — only to disagree. Others, like Erik Gunnar Asplund and Sigurd Lewerentz, who could well have been expected to join after the hugely successful Stockholm Exhibition and their adherence to the manifesto *Acceptera*, never attended any of the congresses. One of the most eloquent critics at that stage was Eileen Gray, writing in the most important periodical of the time, *L'Architecture Vivante*, which was published by Jean Badovici. Confronted by the assertion that standardisation and industrial building methods were a necessity brought about by economic circumstances, she replied:

> It is essential not to present as Ideal something which is simply the result of unfortunate necessity.... It's always the same story: technology ends up as the principal preoccupation. The end is forgotten by thinking only of the means.... We must build for people so that they can find once more in architecture the joy of enlarged powers and self-fulfilment.[15]

Hans Scharoun
Schminke House, Löbau, 1933.
Garden facade and living room.

In the event, a significant number of independent architects all over the world proceeded in their own way to produce work widely ranging in kind, but all in terms of Practical Art, deriving form from purpose and placing "Man at the centre".[16] It constituted a body of work that self-evidently matched Haering's criteria of making buildings that responded to "the way things wanted to be". Aalto once said: "What matters is not what a building looks like when it is new but what it looks like 30 years later." 60 and 70 years later we find these buildings still in prime condition, still enjoyed in terms of their original purpose, still loved by their inhabitants. This is not a claim that can be lodged by many of the orthodox members of the Congress. It is, however, a claim that in itself has gained the authority to merit the status of an Other Tradition.

It is that claim which merits a hearing.

Hans Scharoun
Schminke House, Löbau, 1933.
Wintergarden.

NOTES—CHAPTER ONE

1   Lissitzsky, El and Hans Arp, *The Isms*, Zurich: Eugen Reutsch Verlag, 1925.
2   Peter Behrens, Victor Bourgeois, Le Corbusier and Pierre Jeanneret, Richard Döcker, Josef Frank, Walter Gropius, Ludwig Hilbersheimer, Mies van der Rohe, JJP Oud, Hans Poelzig, Adolf Rading, Hans Scharoun, Adolf Schneck, Mart Stam, Bruno Taut, Max Taut.
3   Gropius, Walter, *Internationale Architektur*, Weimar: Bauhaus, 1925; Hilberseimer, L, *Internationale Neue Baukunst*, Hoffmann, 1928; Badovici, J, *L'Architecture Vivante*, 1923–1933, 22 vols.
4   Sert, JL, *Can our Cities Survive?*, Cambridge, MA: Harvard University Press, 1942, p. ix.
5   First Manifesto of CIAM, La Sarraz, 28 June, 1928.
6   First Manifesto of CIAM.
7   I am indebted to Peter Blundell-Jones for this information.
8   Hudnut, Dean, Introduction to *Can our Cities Survive?*, p. iii.
9   Haering, Hugo, *Wege zur Form*, 1925.
10 Haering, "Probleme des Bauens", *Der Neubau*, trans. Blundell-Jones, Heft no. 17, 10 September, 1924.
11 Haering, *Der Neubau*, ch. 4, part iii.
12 First Manifesto of CIAM.
13 First Manifesto of CIAM.
14 Fishman, Robert, "From the Radiant City to Vichy", in *The Open Hand*, Cambridge, MA: MIT Press, 1977.
15 Dialogue "From Eclecticism to Doubt", Badovici/Gray, in *L'Architecture Vivante*, Albert Morance, Autumn 1929, p. 20.
16 A representative list of names of first generation Modernists of the Other Tradition would include: Adolf Loos, Erik Gunnar Asplund, Sigurd Lewerentz, Alvar Aalto, Erik Bryggmann, Franco Albini, Ignazio Gardella, Frank Lloyd Wright, Rudolf Schindler, Johannes Duiker, Bernard Bijvoet, Hans Scharoun, Hugo Haering, Bruno Taut, Ernst May, Erich Mendelsohn, Rudolf Schwarz, Eileen Gray, Luis Barragán, Carlo Scarpa.

CHAPTER TWO

THE SECOND EPISODE
THE INVENTION OF 'THE INTERNATIONAL STYLE'

Architecture has at last been freed from
the ossification that is the fate of 'Style'.

JB VAN LOGHEM

Bouwen/Bauen/Bâtir/Building, 1932.

The next stage in the growing paralysis that stemmed from CIAM came from a different source altogether. It was an attempt at popularisation brought about by two 'tourists' from New York avid to pin down (in the tradition of the Grand Tour) the challenging story of what had been going on in Europe.

In 1930, Alfred Barr, director of the newly founded Museum of Modern Art (MoMA) in New York, commissioned Henry-Russell Hitchcock and Philip Johnson — genially described by Frank Lloyd Wright in his breezy way as "a self advertising amateur and a high powered salesman" — to investigate the 'new' architecture that was springing up in Europe and to bring back a report on its 'style'.[1] The bogey-word at that time was 'Functionalism', and Barr suggested that what they were seeking might well be called 'Post-Functionalism'; certainly the sole criteria to be applied was aesthetic — the search for a new style.[2] Philip Johnson wrote to his mother: "No one wants another book on modern architecture here in Germany.... In vain do we explain that there has been no book covering the whole style and nothing but the style."[3]

And so, disregarding the real tensions and irresolutions in the situation that they encountered, Johnson and Hitchcock returned with a 'style' to order, and this they called "The International Style". In 1932 their book, the MoMA exhibition and its catalogue duly crowned the event.

As is the wont of 'styles', a neat set of rules was deployed and these can be counted on the fingers of one hand — four fingers to be exact:

1. The first rule called for volume 'as opposed to mass and solidity'
2. The second called for 'regularity rather than symmetry'
3. The third called for the 'avoidance of applied decoration'
4. The fourth declared that 'symbolic expression by allusion to the past... has ceased to be necessary'.

[A rider to this proposition is the fact that the syllabus of the Bauhaus excluded the history of architecture: in Gropius' words: "Modern Architecture is not a few branches of an old tree — it is a new growth coming right from the roots."]

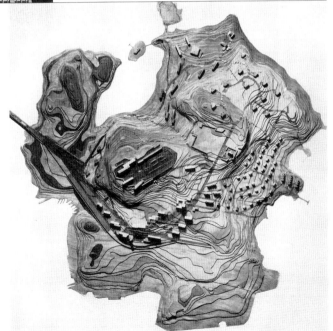

<u>TOP</u>:
Philip Johnson
AT&T Building
New York, 1984.

<u>BOTTOM</u>:
Alvar Aalto
Säynätsalo, 1949.
Model of the layout
of the island.

The amateur vagueness of this list of criteria is cruelly exposed when compared to the incisiveness of Le Corbusier's 1926 "Five Points of Architecture", in which the correlation between new technical, formal and functional potentialities was made explicit and drawn together to form a precise and canonical set of rules. But then we also have to note that Le Corbusier's exegesis was prefaced by the statement, "we are totally uninterested in aesthetic fantasies or attempts at fashionable gimmicks". We may have reason to doubt the strict sincerity of that profession, but it is expressive of a commonly held view at that time in Europe. We should therefore not be surprised to find that if we look at another book, also published in 1932, but written from the European standpoint, we get a very different picture. JB Van Loghem's *Bouwen/Bauen/Bâtir/Building* carried the subtitle *Vers une architecture réelle* (*An architecture for living in*) — a concept never touched upon in the values of our tourists. "Architecture has at last been freed from 'Style', that is to say from the ossification that is the fate of 'Style'".[4] 'Style', for Van Loghem, was the by-product of getting a great number of quite other issues right. It was a reward: it could never be the starting point. Johnson's proud claim that the significance of his and Hitchcock's research lay in the fact that they were unique in focusing upon "the whole Style and nothing but the Style" is eloquently demonstrated by a comparison between his and Van Loghem's caption to the facade of Le Corbusier's Villa at Garches. To Van Loghem it is a demonstration of "the destruction of the facade". Johnson simply comments "one wall is grey and one green to emphasise the planes". Hitchcock had already revealed his obsession with the concept of style in his *Modern Architecture* of 1929, in which he wrote that "each style *(sic)* of architecture is able to express certain functions perfectly.... Only by a loss of perfect integrity can a style succeed in giving the most adequate expression to all the functions." To the aesthete, integrity is owed to expression rather than to the demands (so messy) of life.

One major by-product of the International Style publications and exhibitions was the finding of teaching posts in the USA for Gropius, Breuer, Mies and Hilbersheimer; the uprooting of these leading members of the CIAM orthodoxy from the continuing debate in Europe, together with the exodus of the Communist group to Russia, left Le Corbusier without any rival of any significance within the CIAM establishment.

The year before the meeting at La Sarraz, Alvar Aalto wrote: "We cannot create new form where there is no new content."[5] If there is one working principle that is common to all of the architects of the Resistance, it is this: purposive form is generated from inside out. To seek to freeze the forms that develop out of such a mode into a canon is irrational; to impose that canon as a mould into which any kind of content can then be shoehorned is simply a contradiction in terms. The process is not reversible. But this is exactly what happened with the invention of the International Style. The inauthenticity of the operation produced work of unredeemable banality: as a 'style' it was condemned at birth.

JB van Loghem
Bouwen, Bauen, Bâtir, Building,
cover, 1932.
Not "architecture" but "built to live in".

"The International Style."

TOP:
Otto Haesler
Block of flats,
Kassel, 1930.

BOTTOM:
Mamoru Yamada
Electricity laboratory,
Tokyo, 1929.

To understand this point, one has only to compare the vitality of a building by Johannes Duiker who, significantly, was not included in the selection of buildings for *The International Style* exhibition with a number of the carthorses that were. It was inevitable that as the impulse to generate the real thing became more outweighed and outnumbered by the next generation of International Style buildings, boredom would set in. There is an inherent obligation to think up something new, to be original. It is significant that this compulsion is absent from the values of the Other Tradition where new ground is broken only where new need demands it.

To the aesthete and the follower of fashion, nothing can be more unforgivable than to be boring, for boredom is to the aesthete what acedia was to the monks.

And so, eventually, Philip Johnson, ever eager to amuse, stepped back onto the stage and announced the birth of a new 'style' — not 'Post-Functionalism' this time, but 'Post-Modernism'. The four rules for this 'style' were as follows:
1. The first rule called for 'mass' rather than volume
2. The second for bilateral symmetry rather than regularity
3. The third for the return of decoration
4. The fourth for symbolic expression to be pre-eminent.

Historical reference was now to be part of the game of lucky dip — a particularly seductive proposition for those who had been denied such 'fun' by Gropius both at the Bauhaus and at Harvard.

One only has to notice that these criteria are simply the reverse of the rules for the International Style, to realise that no great creative energy went into their formulation and that their sole motivation was aesthete's boredom. Nothing could demonstrate more clearly the sickly inbreeding that infects a sole preoccupation with 'style'. This particular exercise has been succinctly described by the philosopher Jürgen Habermas as the quest for "re-enchantment [by] the avant-garde of the Great Retreat".

It is very significant that, at this time, the Museum of Modern Art mounted a major exhibition on the Ecole des Beaux-Arts — an influence never far below the surface in American architecture; and with it came, inevitably, a return to "the Battle of the Styles".[6]

TOP AND BOTTOM:
Alvar and Aino Aalto
Villa Mairea,
Noormarkku,
1937–1939.
Entrance facade
and sauna.

To the architects of the Other Tradition, history had never been a subject to be dismissed. Association, reference and symbolic form were always part of the discourse in their work. Part of the 'play' in Aalto's Villa Mairea was the explicit weaving together of themes from Purism to traditional Karelian vernacular. This architecture suffered in no way from the absence of historical reference or formal sophistication that Postmodernism claimed to be re-introducing. And it is not difficult to see that the response to historic form by Asplund in the 1930s was far more learned and inventive than any of the Postmodern gestures. The architecture of the Other Tradition had no need for redemption or "re-enchantment" by the Postmodern entertainers.

Gunnar Asplund
Gothenburg Law Courts,
1934–1937.

Frank Lloyd Wright
Johnson Wax Headquarters,
Racine, 1936–1939.

As early as 1935, Aalto pointed out that Modernism and the dead hand of the Academy "had grown closer and together form a large formalist front in opposition to a rational view of life and art".7 It is also significant, but not surprising, that his work and, to a greater extent, that of Scharoun and Haering, was from the time of the publication of *The International Style* persistently marginalised by Hitchcock by being identified as "Expressionist", and by Giedion as "irrational". It is interesting to note Hitchcock's uneasiness about Aalto when he came to write a foreword to the 1966 reprint of *The International Style*. In discussing the choice of 1932 as the key date for the publication he argued that 1929 would have been too soon for enough built evidence to be available (since "architecture is always a set of actual monuments, not a vague corpus of theory"). On the other hand, 1936 would have been too late, since by then "Aalto and a rejuvenated Frank Lloyd Wright" were "sharply changing the international picture". And the very fact that this phenomenon of 'Post-Modernism' could so easily capture the amount of attention that it did, is proof itself that the focus upon 'style' had not been seriously challenged, after all, by the members of CIAM itself; rather, it had compounded its own original error by drawing down upon its head yet further error. In doing so, it had successfully diverted attention from the central issue — Van Loghem's "architecture for living in", which Hugo Haering had tried in vain to present at La Sarraz.

NOTES—CHAPTER TWO

1   Riley, Terence, and Stephen Perella, *The International Style: Exhibition 15 at the Museum of Modern Art*, New York: Rizzoli, 1992.
2   Foreword to *The International Style: Architecture Since 1922*, HR Hitchcock and Philip Johnson, New York: WW Norton, 1932.
3   Riley and Perella, *The International Style: Exhibition 15 at the Museum of Modern Art*, p. 14.
4   Van Loghem, JB, *Bowen/Bauen/Bâtir/Building*, Amsterdam: Kosmos, 1932.
5   Schildt, G, *Alvar Aalto: The Decisive Years*, New York: Rizzoli, 1986, p. 226.
6   *The Architecture of the Ecole des Beaux-Arts*, exhibition at MoMA, New York, October 1975–January 1976.
7   Aalto, Alvar, "Rationalism and Man", in *Sketches*, Cambridge, MA: MIT Press, 1978, p. 47.

DOCTRINE

CHAPTER THREE

CLASSICAL THEORY AND THE AESTHETIC FALLACY

It is in changing that things repose.

HERACLITUS

Fragment 23.

In order to appreciate the architectural values and prejudices prevailing at any one time, it is helpful to plot their relationship for purposes of comparison with the order of values that we attribute to the Classical tradition.

But as soon as that is said we are reminded of TS Eliot's warning that tradition itself is not a fixed order of values:

> What happens when a new work of art is created is something that happens simultaneously to all the works of art which preceded it. The existing monuments form an ideal order among themselves, which is modified by the introduction of the new (the really new) work of art among them. The existing order is complete before the new work arrives; for order to persist after the supervention of novelty, the whole existing order must be, if ever so slightly, altered.[1]

How, then, do we establish a viable account of the Classical tradition of architecture?

In the first place we have to make a distinction between, on the one hand, its superficial connotation as a 'style', and on the other its special place as an art form grounded in Classical Greek philosophy. Since, as we shall see, the claim that it is a 'style' (and above all a 'timeless style' limited to the use of the Orders) is rooted in ignorance of the philosophy, we would do well to address the philosophy first.

Emmanuel Pontremoli
The Acropolis of Pergamon
reconstructed.

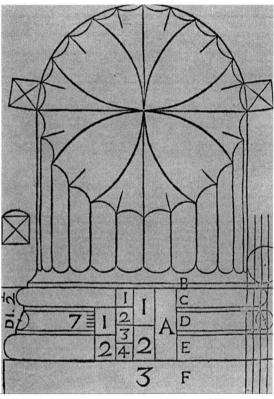

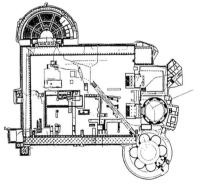

<u>TOP LEFT</u>:
Sebastiano Serlio
The Five Orders.

<u>TOP RIGHT</u>:
Guiseppe Viola Zanini
Correct Rules of the Five Orders.

<u>BOTTOM</u>:
Sanctuary of Asklepios,
Pergamon.

The fact that a fundamental ignorance of Classical values does indeed prevail today can be demonstrated by reference to a number of issues. The most crucial of these is the lamentable separation of the roles of 'art' and 'function' as if they were in opposition to each other, whereas the very essence of Classical thought insisted on their fusion. Indeed, in order to renew our understanding of the Classical view we will above all need to understand how the divorce of these two terms came about.

We would therefore be well advised to go to the origins of the theory of architecture that we have inherited within the tradition of Western culture. Its formulation is founded in a set of principles propounded by the Greek 'ancients' and subsequently glossed by the Romans, the Mediaeval schoolmen and the scholar-architects of the Renaissance.

This whole structure of thought has been built up from a cluster of propositions drawn from various sources in Classical Greek philosophy. Unfortunately, the original treatises do not exist. Vitruvius refers to at least seven original Greek texts but, alas, none of them have survived.[2] And so we have to reconstruct that scaffold from hints offered by Vitruvius himself — mumbled fragments and half-remembered formulae — and relate these to what we do know of principles enunciated by the philosophers.

The first of those principles hinges upon Aristotle's distinction between two kinds of art: 'Fine Art', "whose end is to serve only itself", and 'Practical Art', "that serves an end other than itself". The Greeks, who found a way of embodying in metaphor every nuance of the human psyche and who peopled the world of elements and passions with a hierarchy of 835 deities, who gave us the Orders and the departure from the Orders, the Parthenon and Hagia Sophia, scarcely mention architecture in all their literature — Plato and Aristotle not a word, and Homer little better; and in the roll-call of the nine Muses they accorded no place to it. Nor did they call architecture 'the Mother of the Arts' — a piece of ignorance that seems to have found its way into common parlance. (The Mother of the Arts was Memory, *Mnemosyne*.) This was no oversight of the Greek ancients but, on the contrary, a precise reflection of their insistence that building is one of the Practical Arts: its 'art' lay not in the pursuit of art for art's sake but in serving quite another end. In the words of Aristotle, "the virtue of a thing is related to its proper function".

What, then, is the "end" that is served by this Practical Art? The Greek concept of *telos* proposed that there is a unique purposefulness inherent in all created things and that it is the flowering and fulfilment of its potential powers that is the moving force in nature and in all human enterprise. We desire such fulfilment, and our enjoyment of life (*Eudaimonia*) lies in its achievement.

For this reason, Classical theory demands first and foremost a clear apprehension of the ultimate end, or *causa finalis*, that the work is to serve. Therefore architecture's first cause, its origin and its inspiration, is to realise some desirable end that can only be fulfilled by a building.

Clearly related to this concept of inbuilt purpose (*telos*) is the notion of necessity (*anagke*) which is the outer constraint imposed upon the fulfilment of all things. To Alberti, writing in the fifteenth century, architecture is "born of necessity and nurtured by use".[3] It is the task of a Practical Art to make, out of the constraints of necessity, a vehicle for the fulfilment of desire. And so behind the Classical concept of form there lies the concept of 'play' as the element that raises the necessary to the status of the significant, giving to the formless a form that structures the necessary events and imprints upon the minds of those who perceive it a vivid and enjoyable identity. In the words of Plato, "life must be lived as play", which the poet Schiller glossed as "man is only truly man when he is playing" (*homo ludens*).[4]

What we mean when we say that architecture has the power to transcend necessity is well illustrated by the account written by Goethe (in the journal of his visit to Verona) of the occasion in which he came to wonder how and why the great amphitheatre in Verona ever came into existence.[5] In doing so his thoughts went back to the time when there was no amphitheatre. In the event of a public spectacle occurring, people would be driven to use what devices they could to see over the heads of those in front of them: standing on tubs, on wagons, on improvised platforms, and in this way creating a bowl of spectacle that was later translated by architecture into a new entity that came to be called "amphitheatre". Out of a shambles, architecture gave rise to a monument, bringing structure not only to an edifice but also to the behaviour and self-awareness of a society. It taught a community how to celebrate the entertainment of spectacle and made of the occasion a building form that has inspired a whole progeny of successors throughout the world.

– 06

Next we have to enquire how we can discover the specific nature of the "end" or cause to be served in each case — the *causa finalis*. Here we have to recognise that it is not easy to know in any given situation what are the true and most beneficial objectives to be pursued. The Classical concept of the 'true' (*aletheia*) is of an entity whose nature is secretive and is, by definition, concealed beneath the surface of appearances. In the words of Heraclitus, "Nature loves to hide"; it has to be drawn out and made to reveal itself.[6] It follows, therefore, that the origin of any work of architecture lies, in the first place, in a process of discovering the proper end to be served in a particular context of desires and necessities. It is the discovery of an obligation. A Practical Art always has promises to keep; in the sense in which it is answerable to a way of life, architecture is grounded in the ethical.

Insofar then as architecture is Practical, its role will be to provide the technical means by which that desired form will be brought about. The Classical term *methexis* defines the powers that enable something to happen or come into being: it is the quintessential term prevailing in the world of Practical Art. In its activism it is to be contrasted with *mimesis* which is the concern to copy a pre-existing model — a static concept which more properly prevails in the world of Fine Art. When the end has been determined it will be the task of architecture to invent the form that will match all the requirements — the *causa formalis*.

TOP:
Choisy
Greek column and beam
temple architecture.

BOTTOM:
The Temple at Paestum.

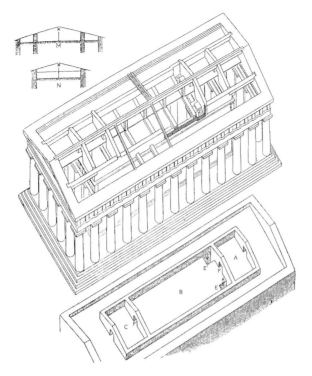

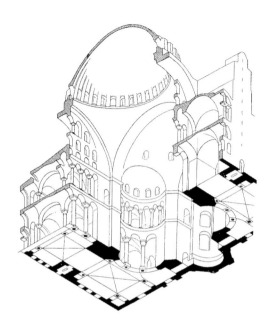

Finally, the means that are unique to architecture and which scholars defined as the third cause — *causa materialis* — lie self-evidently in the art of making (*poiesis*). Within the discipline of building this took the form of *tektonik*.

And so we see that the Classical ethos requires of architectural design a strict linear sequence that proceeds from the discovery of what is desirable to the invention of an appropriate form, and thence to the elaboration of the technical means that make it possible. Pursuing that living sequence it can bring a form of life to its full identity for the first time, vivid and memorable.

This is the Classical definition of architecture. It is not a stylistic prescription, for it is not confined to any one language of forms. The Orders were invented by Greek architects in the fourth century BC, explicitly for the creation of temples dedicated to mythical figures. To that end the concept is specific. But it is as narrow as it is powerful, and certainly it is a denial of the openness to novel experience that is necessary to "serve" with propriety a limitless extension of "ends" beyond tomb-worship. For proof of that we see how Greek architects themselves were the first to go beyond that range of forms when they built Hagia Sophia. To serve the needs of a huge congregation they invented a syntax of dome, vault, pendentive and buttress — vast and apparently weightless volumes brimming with light that bore no kinship whatsoever to the trabeated construction and dark cell of the temple form. New content; another language.

TOP:
Choisy
Greek Byzantine vault
and dome construction
for Hagia Sofia,
Istanbul.

BOTTOM:
Hagia Sofia, Istanbul.

It is above all a *modus operandi* whose supreme insight was to insist upon the unconditional fusion of purpose and means, *telos* matched by *tektonik* (in that order), invention responding to desire. This is exactly the opposite of art for art's sake (Fine Art), and it led then to a concept which summarised in one term (*to kalon*) the notions of purpose and beauty. This concept was so taken for granted that it was seen to be ordinary (*banausos*), and that very confidence in its normality carried the further significance of public assent, of an agreement won out of some form of participation in the discovery of what is desirable in each context.

We no longer have such a concept in our vocabulary. It was destroyed in the eighteenth century following the invention by Kant and his followers of the concept of 'aesthetics'. In his *Critique of Judgement*, Kant defined the essence of the work of art in terms of "purposefulness without purpose", and this idea was pursued to a further point of purposelessness in the Sublime whose nature was, among other things, positively to defy not only the normal but even the very notion of purpose at the root of art.[7]

Architecture, together with all the other arts, was swept into the category of Fine Art — namely a 'pure' art whose sole end was to serve itself: art for art's sake. The inclusion of architecture in this category is virtually a contradiction in terms, and it is significant that the purest advocate of the Sublime, Etienne-Louis Boullée, complained throughout his life that he had not devoted himself to painting alone. Kant himself acknowledged that the notion of the "purposeless" could not apply to architecture, conceding that "for an architectural work it is the suitability of a product for a certain use that is the essential thing".[8]

His discrimination however was disregarded. Beauty and efficiency which, in the Greek mind, had been fused into the one term (*to kalon*) were now torn apart to confront each other. At one blow the central tenet of Classical thought was shattered. One confusion led to another and soon a class distinction entered common parlance in the form of a confrontation between 'architecture' on the one hand and 'building' on the other — a concern for 'beauty' as if it were something to be opposed to a concern for 'mere use'.

TOP
LEFT AND RIGHT:
Etienne-Louis Boullée
Newton Memorial.
Exterior and interior.

BOTTOM:
Marie-Joseph Peyre
Building to contain
the Academies.

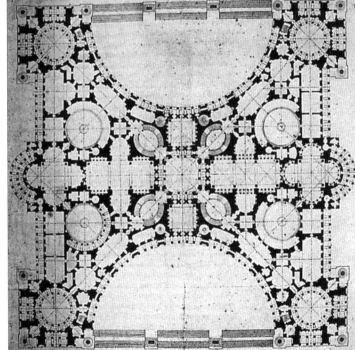

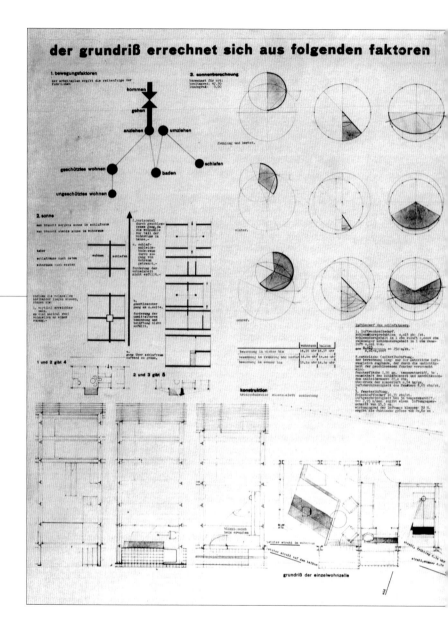

**Students of
Hannes Meyer**
The plan generated
from the logical
sequence of factors.

Inevitably, the advocates of 'architecture' became more and more extreme in the pursuit of art for art's sake and finally reduced the subject to "the Battle of the Styles". At exactly the same time the practice of teaching architecture in an academy rather than in the workshop was developing far and wide and was universally modelled upon the method and syllabus of the Ecole des Beaux-Arts, the values of which were drawn directly from the aesthetics of the Sublime. At a single stroke a 'paper architecture' that never had to be built and which was dedicated to some irrational 'Sublime' was given the exalted status of the *Grand Prix*, and a new profession was founded upon the pursuit of the purposeless by the impractical. By a fundamental subversion of values, the significance of the design process was shifted away from the search for the true necessities inherent in each request for a building, to focus upon the ingenuity of the designer to shuffle the paper pattern clichés he had up his sleeve.

Charles Percler
Building to contain the Academies.

Not surprisingly, the practicalities of building were devolved upon the separate discipline of engineering that was emerging at the same time out of a rapidly developing science of statics and the analysis of the physical properties of materials. As the Rationalism of the Enlightenment hardened into Positivism, so a nucleus of reaction against the aesthetes began to form in utilitarian terms and the concept of Functionalism emerged as a counterblast. This was not couched in the balanced terms of Classical *telos*. Instead the concept of purposefulness was traduced by being simultaneously elevated in status but narrowed in focus to 'the measurable' — to diagrams of operational performance and limits of structural performance. "I taught my students... to come to grips with the only reality that can be mastered — that of the measurable, the visible, the weighable."[9] The goal of enjoyment in a way of doing things was reduced analytically to the execution of a task. The sensibility that was tuned to an art that celebrated the practical (a sensibility that had remained intact to the end of the eighteenth century) was split into two — the twin follies of 'architecture for architecture's sake' and 'Functionalism'. The split became an invitation to fly to extreme simplifications. On the one hand, 'building' could be seen to have "nothing to do with art at all" in the famous definition of Hannes Meyer ("architecture = function x economics").[10] Even in the graphic presentation of his work he attempts to make a brilliant design look like a standard application for a patent! On the other hand, to the high priests of aesthetics, the concepts of purpose, use and *telos* were denigrated as 'mere utility' and architecture was to be viewed as 'autonomous' — answerable only to its own set of rules.

TOP AND BOTTOM:
**Hannes Meyer
and Hans Wittwer**
Peter's School, Basle, 1926.
Perspective and competition
submission.

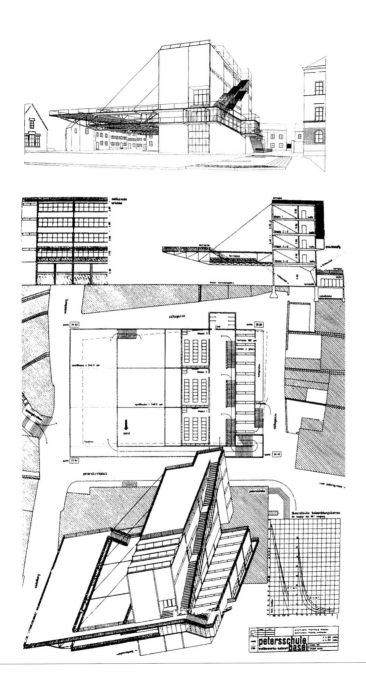

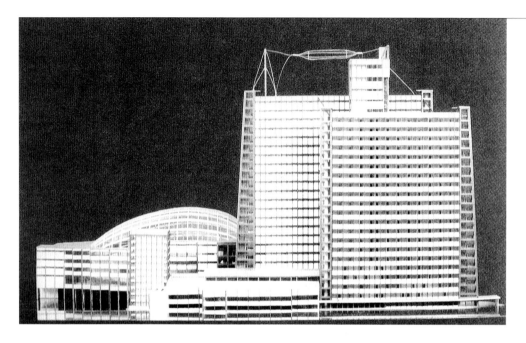

Hannes Meyer
Project for the League
of Nations, 1927.

And so in our search for the origins of Classical architectural theory we have paradoxically come to retrieve the concept of 'function' from 'Functionalism' and the concept of Classical architecture from its confinement to a dead language — the 'Orders' (whitewashed).

It is an unexpected consequence of the attempt to define the Other Tradition that we must, in the first place, root out the fallacy that has thrived upon the false polarity 'art versus function' and thereby to re-affirm the original but long-lost Classical principle of unity in which the two concepts were one thing in the name of a Practical Art.

Indeed, it has become quite clear that what has been heralded as the 'innovation' within the Modern Movement — namely the emphasis upon functionality — is in fact the renaissance of the oldest Classical principle of all: *to kalon*. In its origin, the Modern Movement was truly a renaissance — not of forms but of fundamental intention.

NOTES—CHAPTER THREE

1 Eliot, TS, "Tradition and the Individual Talent", in *The Sacred Wood*, London: Methuen, 1920.
2 570–560 BC   Theodorus and Rhoecus treatise on the Heraeum at Samos.
   570–560 BC   Chersiphron and Metagenes on the Temple of Artemis at Ephesus.
   375 BC   Philo of Eleusis.
   175 BC   Hermogenes (cf Vitruvius, Preface to Book VII).
                 Silenus on the Doric.
                 Pythius on the Ionic Temple of Minerva, Priene.
                 Ictinus and Carpion: Doric Temple of Minerva on The Acropolis.
                 Theodorus of Phocaea: on the Tholos at Delphi.
                 Arcesius: on Corinthian proportion and Ionic Temple at Tralles Satyrus and Pythius on the Mausoleum.
                 "Many volumes by the Greeks" (Frigidius).
3 Alberti, LB, *Ten Books on Architecture*, book 1, ch. IX.
4 Plato, *Laws*, viii 803; Schiller, Friedrich, Letter XV, *On the Aesthetic Education of Man*, London: Routledge & Kegan Paul Ltd, 1954.
5 Fairely, Barker, *A Study of Goethe*, Oxford: Oxford University Press, 1947.
6 Heraclitus, *Fragment 17*.
7 Kant, Immanuel, *Critique of Judgement*, part 1, Second Moment, paragraph 10.
8 Kant, *Critique of Judgement*, Fourth Moment.
9 Meyer, Hannes, "Marxist Architecture" 1931, in *Hannes Meyer: Buildings, Projects and Writings*, Claude Schnaidt ed., London: Tiranti, 1963.
10 Meyer, *Buildings, Projects and Writings*, Claude Schnaidt ed., London: Tiranti, 1963.

CHAPTER FOUR

THE OTHER IDEA
ARCHITECTURE AS A PRACTICAL ART

The art of High Utility.

WR LETHABY

in "Form in Civilisation", *Collected papers on Art and Labour.*

THE QUESTION OF ORIGIN

We have referred to the way in which the establishment of the teaching methods of the Ecole des Beaux-Arts became universal practice in the setting up of the first schools of architecture. It is necessary therefore to give some account of the nature of these methods and the values that they pursued, since it will become apparent that both were profoundly subversive of Classical practice with respect to the proper sources from which any design should draw its priorities.

We should therefore look hard at the actual procedures adopted in the studios of the Ecole des Beaux-Arts. In the first place these were exclusively framed with a view to developing the students' 'powers of imagination'. This was, of course, particularly suited to addressing ideas of the Sublime. In order to test the students' aptitude in this field, an extraordinary routine was devised. The general type of building to be designed would be announced (a hospital, a theatre, a library, etc.) so that some very general research (usually into precedents) could be carried out, but no specific facts about size or content would be given, nor any indication of the nature of the site. All such information was withheld until the holding of the examination itself when the students would be locked into the studio (*en loge*) for one day during which they were required to prepare their sketch-scheme (*esquisse*) establishing the principal features of their design (the *parti*). No departure from that *parti* was permitted in subsequent work, no matter how much new information had been gleaned in the meantime or how many second thoughts had stormed the brain; and all further work for the rest of the year took the form of developing that first inspiration. The fundamental work — a 12 hour 'test of the imagination' — was signed and sealed: all that was left were the details. No dialogue was allowed — no answers to questions, no discussion with client, occupant, or specialist — either with a view to better understanding the brief or to the criticism of alternative proposals; no visit to site, research into the historical context; and no development of technical feasibility.

Hans Scharoun
Initial sketches
for the Philharmonie,
Berlin.

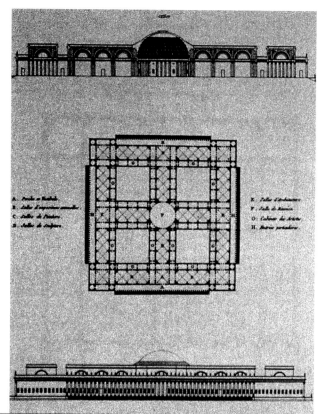

Jean-Nicolas-Louis Durand
Design for a Museum, 1805.
Précis, 1805.
Typical floor plans/course
diagrams for the Ecole
Polytechnique.

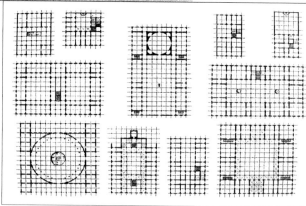

As a way of creating an exercise in paper patterns this procedure is
not unreasonable and, indeed, where the end in view is an exercise in the
Sublime, it is quite appropriate. But as the mode of origin of a piece of
architecture — a work of Practical Art — it is deeply perverse. And yet
it became an unchallenged practice in schools of architecture throughout
the world.

It is furthermore ironic that the compositional rules evolved at the Ecole
(*distribution*, *symétrie*, *circulation*, *poché*, *mosaïque*) for purposes of bringing
order to the imagination were shortly taken over by Durand at the Ecole
Polytechnique as counters in a desiccated game played out, like chess, on a
grid of coordinates. What the grand manner of the Ecole des Beaux-Arts
offered to Le Corbusier in his compositional games, the design-kit of the
Ecole Polytechnique offered a pragmatic modus operandi for the neutral
Rationalism pursued by the Miesians post-Second World War.

Arthur Takeuchi Wendell
Elementary School,
Chicago, 1972-1973.
Typical grid floor plan.

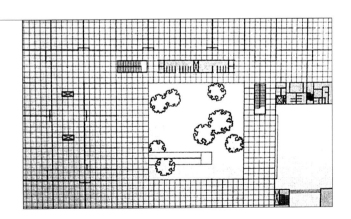

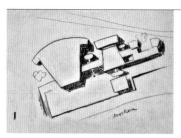

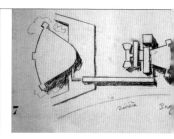
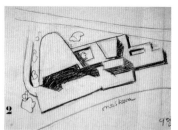
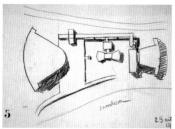
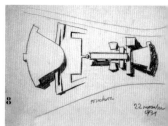
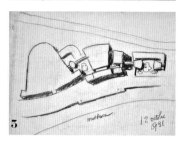
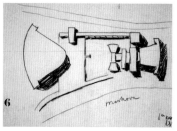

Le Corbusier
Palace of the Soviets,
Moscow, 1930.
Compositional studies.

The peculiar nature of the work of the Ecole was ostensibly the grounds for protest by the founding fathers of the Modern Movement: for instance, Le Corbusier's response to the invitation to teach at the Ecole des Beaux-Arts was to say that the whole institution should be razed to the ground and salt sprinkled on the site as a ritual of purification![1] But rooted ideas are not so easily eliminated and, as we shall see, there was a lot more of the *esprit de L'Ecole* in Le Corbusier's philosophy than he was prepared to admit. Indeed, in describing the virtues of the plan whose "elegance of solution" is due to "eminently French values, unknown anywhere else", he goes on to say that "the Ecole des Beaux-Arts... would emerge victorious if its aims were other than constantly striking effects reached by graphic methods which invariably lead to Orsay Stations and Grand Palais".[2]

This has direct bearing on the principle upon which Haering fell out with Le Corbusier and which is summed up in his plea that "we must examine things and allow them to unfold their own forms".[3] For Le Corbusier the forms did not have to be discovered; they already existed in his head. The geometry of Purism, the technology of the frame structure and the canon of the "Five Points of Architecture" which he had set out for their ordonnance in 1926 had settled that matter once and for all. Life was to be played out in accordance with the rules of "a knowing and correct play of forms in light"; and every building was to be made into the occasion for a demonstration of the virtues of that canon.[4] The project in question may not be a commission at all but rather the self-instigated illustration or particular application of this thesis. It might be the exploration of a new building type (the Radiant Farm) or the formal device by which a building might grow over time in a consistent way (the spiral of the Museum of Continuous Growth) or an example of the *promenade architecturale* (demonstrated in the Villa Stein). Always the ultimate goal was the 'harmony' to be derived from the contemplation of that 'knowing and correct play of forms'. What is offered is the demonstration of an idea in the one language that simultaneously appeals to the mind and the senses — geometry. Its appeal to the intellect (*la satisfaction de L'Esprit*) lies precisely in the fact that it is the one visual language that has that power. Nobody in the twentieth century brought such intelligence, originality and sheer formal mastery to the invention of the work of architecture as an object of geometrical exactitude — as a work of Fine Art. It is indeed magnificent, but it is no answer to Haering's question.

And not only in Haering's mind.

As we have already seen between the publication of the "Five Points" and the debate at La Sarraz, Alvar Aalto had written: "We cannot create new form where there is no new content."[5] It is clear that for both him and Haering the origin of form lies in response to the desire for a certain form of life, not in the fusion between a way of painting and a way of building, however inspired. To ask of any situation not only what is required but what is desired is to ask a hard question. It is hard for two reasons: firstly because you do not at first know whom to ask or how; and secondly because the answer may not be what you were hoping for. But it is the only way to get a living response and certainly the only way in which to rescue the notion of 'purpose' from 'mere utility'.

Le Corbusier's own response is typical of the aesthete. Quite simply he evades the issue of utility by continuing to see it not in terms of living, of the joyful fulfilment of purpose, but by juxtaposing it to 'beauty', there by dragging the whole issue back into the safe ground of aesthetics once more. In a famous exchange with the Czech Functionalist, Karel Teige, he illustrates the hoary antithesis 'utility versus beauty' by an episode in his office:

> Last year, upon completion of the drawings of the Mundaneum project there was a minor revolt in our studio. The younger members of the group criticized the pyramid (which is one of the elements of the project). On other drawing boards, the drawings of the Centrosoyus for Moscow were just being finished and had received everyone's approval. They were reassuring because that scheme was clearly a rational problem of an office building. Nevertheless, the Mundaneum and the Centrosoyus both emerged from our heads during the same month of June.
>
> All of a sudden the decisive argument popped out of a mouth: "What is useful is beautiful!" At the same moment Alfred Roth (of such impetuous temperament) kicked in the side of a wire mesh wastebasket which couldn't hold the quantity of old drawings he was trying to stuff in. Under Roth's energetic pressure, this wastebasket, which had a technically

'sachlich' curvature (a direct expression of the wire netting), deformed and took on the appearance shown in the sketch above. Everyone in the office roared. "It's awful", said Roth. "Ah, but this basket now contains much more", I replied, "it is more useful so we could say it is more beautiful! Be consistent with your principles!"[6]

The word 'function' is then simply swallowed up in verbal play and returned once more to the field of aesthetics — "*la fonction fondamentale humaine, qu'est la beauté*": and the building remains the object of contemplation, the work of Fine Art.

Elsewhere in this argument with Karel Teige, he writes that "utilitarian objects" are "ephemeral" and "spiritual ones" are "permanent". The Calvinist in his blood pushes aside the Cartesian. It is as if he is positively insisting that 'the useful' cannot be 'the beautiful' — beauty, like Grace, derives from another source, is of another category, something added not inherent.

On the other hand, Haering's statement takes for granted the assumption that there is an inherent "end other than itself" that the architecture has to serve, and furthermore that the end in question is the satisfaction of a desire for a certain way of living.

It is essential to realise here that we are not addressing crude necessity nor mere utility, but the full-blooded desire for the fulfilment of a certain way of life; and this is a notion that has a much more substantial claim to be called a 'fundamental human function' than some abstract notion of beauty. And rather than sneer at the statement that "what is useful is beautiful", it might be better to consider how it relates to the Classical concept of *to kalon*.

Here we must recall the distinction we have made between 'the necessary' and 'the desirable'. The notion of necessity as an unwelcome chore leads in the mind of the aesthete to the relegation of the acts of daily living to the realm of things to be despised. The ultimate position of the aesthete has been summarised by the disdain of the poet who said "Living? Our servants will do that for us...."[7] For the aesthete, use at once becomes 'mere use'.

To save the concept of use, of purpose, of function from such mindless denigration we have simply to search out and elucidate those aspects of architecture that draw their origin, their order and their identity (their very *quidditas*) from an embeddedness in fulfilling a way of life. We will find that they will all revolve around the difference between the building viewed as an object (the beautiful object contemplated *sub specie aeternitatis*) and the building viewed as a framework for the actions of men, a place of enactment and celebration, a theatre that makes action possible (*methexis*); viewed from without certainly, but above all entered within, experienced existentially, attuned in terms of light and the whole sensorium (touch, smell and hearing), a framework in which, to use the phrase of Aldo van Eyck, "Space becomes Place and Time becomes Occasion."

Insofar as their origin patently grows from a source generated by factors far removed from the discipline of architecture, the desired forms cannot necessarily be drawn from a pre-existing canon; they are by definition unpredictable. At times of significant change in social values this very fact is the source of inspiration that can make possible the discovery and gratification of a desire that could never have been conceived through any other form of genesis.

There is an analogy here to nature in the creation of life through the fusion of diverse identities. For unlike any other work of art, a building does have a life; it engages not only with the ways of men but also endures the laws of statics and the vagaries of weather, not to mention the unpredictable fortunes of its neighbours. The corollary to this is that unless the building is charged at birth with the appetites and potencies proper to its role, it will be repaid in kind — denatured ruthlessly if not actually demolished.

To the delegates at La Sarraz the sheer novelty of the enterprise and the degree of radical shift in attack required of the architect in coming to terms with the urban slum were enormous: a new form of client (the masses without a voice), a new technical environment (the mass-production of the Henry Ford story), and a scale of operations without precedent (*'le problème du grand nombre'*). We have seen that the response that they adopted was modelled upon that of the political revolutionary.[8] As a result, all of the finer shades, as well as the major issues that would, in traditional circumstances, have been resolved by reference to precedent, were now to be confronted *de novo*. This is the quandary of the revolutionary position. The fault of the CIAM delegates lay precisely in their lack of patience, in their eagerness to launch a campaign, in their assertion of a model based upon Cartesian Rationalism and in their belief that redemption lay above all in technology and industrial methodology: in the 'how', not the 'why'.

Revolutionary forms are born of abstract reason, which is impatient of disagreement and much given to the pursuit of single issues, rather than the balanced resolution of contending issues. Blind to all but those attuned to a train of reason, it will tear the web of all other ties. When Haering protested in favour of allowing the new occasions "to unfold their own forms", he was trying to fill the vacuum once filled through consent by creating some forum of discussion calling upon the participation of the local recipients and occupants of the buildings in the appreciation of priorities and conflicting values.

Secondly, Haering's statement calls for unprecedented methods by which to find out, in Louis Kahn's favourite phrase, "What a building wants to be." The objective is not always something self-evident, particularly in times of change; it is probable that it will lie concealed within a tangle of misunderstandings that requires patient elucidation and, like the Greek concept of truth, will have to be drawn out from concealment. Furthermore, when the state of affairs to be clarified is unprecedented, the search for techniques that will achieve the desired revelation will require a special kind of patience. This is no small matter.

Some form of dialogue of the kind that Giancarlo de Carlo was the first to put into practice as "participation with the future inhabitants of the building" is required. For example, in providing a residential neighbourhood for the staff of Matteoti at Terni near Rome, he set up a form of local 'surgery' in which discussions with the future inhabitants took place, models were presented, tested and modified. Decisions about parking, access, size of balcony and room, sound insulation and privacy — all these and many more of the grounds for satisfaction or exasperation — became part of a debate on priorities and trade-offs in which the whole community shared in making decisions in a patiently structured process.[9]

The quality of intervention that is drawn out in response to dialogue is not only more authentic, but much richer in content than that which is inspired by monologue: it is to understand the true factors at play. For by 'factors' we refer to what works in the carrying out of tasks, in the response to specific context, in the creation of appropriate ambience, in the reconciliation of competing goals and forces — all those specificities that we summarise as 'the facts of life' and whose making possible the Greeks summarised in the word *methexis*. A form of design that cannot find the inspiration that is folded within such occasions or, even worse, positively disdains involvement with them is, to borrow Dr Johnson's phrase, "tired of life".

The failure on the part of CIAM to assume this responsibility is one of the underlying issues upon which the challenge of the Other Tradition takes its stand. It is not as if there were no warnings; remember the touching cry of Paul Klee at the Bauhaus: "The people are not with us!" Nor is it as if, even at La Sarraz, there had not been a number of excellent precedents.

Zonnestraal Sanatorium had been built for the Diamond Workers Union by Byvoet and Duiker in close consultation with Van Zutphen and the staff of the Diamond Workers Union. Peter Smithson wrote of this building that it has "a purity and a faith that we find almost too hard to bear" and of Duiker's buildings in general, that they "appear in retrospect to be central to a new sort of society — a new view of society... the Open

LEFT:
Johannes Duiker and Jan van Zutphen
At the opening of Zonnestraal Sanatorium, Hilversum, 1928.
RIGHT:
Ernst May
Bruchfeldstrasse Development, Frankfurt, 1926.

air School, the Sanatorium, the cinema and even perhaps the middle class hotel".[10] Certainly the building was received with enormous acclaim; and this had set a precedent already being pursued, with yet more rigour, by Alvar Aalto at Paimio. And, on a much larger scale, the work of Ernst May in Frankfurt had proven to be extremely popular with the inhabitants and favourably greeted by the press; it is reported that when the great sculptor Aristide Maillol visited Frankfurt in 1930, he was "almost speechless with amazement": "*C'est parfait, il n'y a pas une tache.*"[11]

To anyone closely acquainted with the numberless interrelated issues encountered in the design of low-rent dwellings, the work of Ernst May in Frankfurt constitutes a miracle of balanced judgement, technical innovation, planning ingenuity and economic horse sense — that is to say it precisely addressed the ends it was required to serve in low-income housing. But in addition to that it should be noted that these developments were never simply dormitories — the fate of so much public authority housing. Shops, schools, churches and other community facilities were woven into the fabric of structure and street.

Ernst May
Römerstadt Development, Frankfurt, 1925-1930.

For the majority of the new buildings, including some by other local architects, May's office could establish standards: not only for doors, windows etc. but also for ground plans for different-sized flats and for the space-saving fitted kitchen, designed by Grete Schütte-Lihotzky, known as the 'Frankfurt Kitchen'. Unit furniture designed by Franz Schuster and Ferdinand Kramer was sold to tenants through a non-profit making municipally owned firm; well-designed beds and light fittings were included in a form of local design register.

There were also in many cases centralised heating and hot-water systems, along with some instances of piped radio; kindergartens had been planned. Particular attention was paid to gardens, two special estates being provided for market gardeners; and a standard weekend house was also designed. There was a triple block of forty-three flats for professional women, and an old people's home designed by Stam and Werner Moser.[12]

The dissemination and discussion of this extraordinary enterprise was carried out in a periodical bulletin entitled *Das Neue Frankfurt*.

Compared with the tragicomedy of Le Corbusier's unlettable contemporary housing enterprise at Pessac, it has a merciful sanity and the very normality that propriety would expect in this spectrum of architecture. In such cases new and satisfying forms were already being "allowed to unfold themselves" (in Haering's phrase) from within the heart of a community. These projects were the living evidence for the approach that Haering was seeking to promote.

Architecture is neither the plaything of aesthetes nor the servant of necessity, but the embodiment of a desired way of life; only in the pursuit of that ambition does its true origin lie. This realisation was the first principle that distinguished Haering and the other architects of the Resistance from the authoritarian basis that was already latent in the stance of the CIAM leaders.

Grete Schütte-Lihotzky
The Frankfurt Kitchen, 1926.

THE SCOPE OF ARCHITECTURE

We have seen in our review of the 'aesthetic fallacy', as well as in Le Corbusier's quarrel with Teige, that the application to architecture of Kant's definition of the "purposelessness" of Fine Art soon led to the class distinction between something called 'architecture' and something called 'building'. Hermann Muthesius was the first to bring this argument into focus at the turn of the century with his *Style-Architecture and Building-Art* of 1902, which is the most lucid statement of the distinction.[13] In its popular form the distinction is expressed in Nikolaus Pevsner's catch-phrase — "St Paul's is 'architecture', a garden-shed is 'building'."[14]

In our investigation of the Ecole des Beaux-Arts' interpretation of 'architecture' we have seen how deeply this concept had perverted the Classical sense of the Practical. It is, however, one of those distinctions that has become accepted as obvious until it is challenged. In that sense it is a typical example of the kind of confusion that the philosopher Wittgenstein diagnosed as a self-inflicted wound brought about by the careless use of language.

Wittgenstein's argument has direct application to architecture since it hinges upon use, intention, purposefulness. He pointed out the way language is used contextually in everyday life. The meaning of a particular word is not in itself absolute, but lies in the context of other words intended to carry a certain message; in another context that same word may be used to carry quite a different message. He concludes, therefore, that the meaning lies in the use rather than in some predetermined fixed sense: "Don't ask for the meaning, ask for the use."[15]

If we relate this insight to the definition of architecture as a Practical Art whose purpose is to serve an "end other than itself", then it follows that the meaning of a work of architecture lies in that 'end' which can only be understood by interpreting in each case its purposive 'use'. We need, therefore, to be alert to meanings that, in their full extent, lie in a range of possibilities as wide as life itself — at least as wide as the gap between a shed and a cathedral.

In another context, Wittgenstein helps to extend the argument by a discussion of the significance of affinities. To illustrate the sense in which a family of meanings can maintain a family resemblance over an extraordinarily extended range of examples, he takes the case of:

> the proceedings we call 'games'... board games, card games, ball games, Olympic games and so on: what is common to them all?.... If you look at them you will not see something that is common to *all*, *but...* a complicated network of similarities overlapping and criss-crossing.[16]

To illustrate what he means by "overlapping" he uses the analogy of a thread whose strength "does not reside in the fact that some one fibre runs through its whole length but in the overlapping of those fibres".

> Instead of producing something common to all that we call 'games' I am saying that these phenomena... are *related* to one another in many different ways. And it is because of these relationships that we call them 'games'.[17]

If we transpose this argument from games to architecture we can readily see that the "fibres" of cathedral and garden shed are inexorably bonded together — however long the thread.

To define the full territory of use across which the discipline of architecture is extended from the symbolic to the instrumental we simply have to recognise that we are confronted by a continuum rather than two discontinuous classes of phenomena called 'architecture' and 'building'.

In this way we can see that every building lies at some point in a spectrum of use or range of occasions whose inherent values can be plotted on an imaginary grid that is calibrated in degrees of complexity and significance of purpose between the physical and the metaphysical — a framework for action or an object of contemplation. The closer the purpose of the building lies to the fulfilment of a definable physical function, the simpler it will be to define its use and assess its effectiveness. Conversely, the closer its purpose lies to the symbolic and the metaphysical, the more complex it will be to weigh up its propriety and merits. But at no point across the spectrum can it be said that there is a categorical break between one class and another. Every building task has to be assessed in terms of its proportional composition of physical and metaphysical components, and therein lies its uniqueness.

At this point we have to fault Haering. In his quarrel with Le Corbusier over the imposition of geometrical forms upon a pattern of use that is quite other, he flies to the extreme of excluding geometrical order at all as mere "expression". In defining the nature of 'fulfilment of purpose' he states that "in nature the organs are not there because of their appearance but simply because of their function" and from that point he argues that the unnatural geometric forms are by definition grounded only in "expression" ("only where we create forms according to a special will to expression can we speak of art").[18] But such expression is precisely the role of any work of art (Practical or Fine) that addresses issues lying at the metaphysical end of the spectrum of use — and it would be nonsense to deny the existence of such legitimate use for, for instance, the cathedral just because it is scarcely relevant to the shed. The whole realm of the artificial imagination — of symbolism and allusion — is precisely what distinguishes human culture from animal culture, and the language of architecture is an accepted extension of that discourse. Furthermore, there is a vitality in the dialectic that embraces simultaneously the framing of geometry and the unruly accidents of the organic. There is a place for both.

Certainly there are extreme poles. The vagaries and contradictions of daily life and the necessary interlocking or nesting of irregular specificities — all these pressures have a swarming organic asymmetry that calls for one kind of order. At the domestic scale that order will not only be loaded with family and social associations and symbols but will be dense in the texture of pragmatic detail. On the other hand, the tomb and the monument call for another order — the silent luminous stasis of the timeless, the form to which (in Alberti's phrase) "nothing can be added, nothing taken away". The use and the meaning of these two modes lie at the opposite ends of a spectrum: but across that spectrum they are joined in fine calibrations determined by propriety.

The validity of this claim for the seamlessness of architectural production lies in the fact that this thread of continuity alone confirms the definition of architecture as a Practical Art "that serves an end other than itself", and it is in the discrimination between the various levels of use in terms of propriety and context that the task to be served by any building can be defined and the degree of its success in matching that task can be judged in an objective way.

For the rest, it quite rightly has to answer in terms of the architectural disciplines themselves — it is either well made or not, creates an ordered pattern of use or not, achieves a formal coherence or not. If it has served the end that called it into being in the first place it will have made possible, out of that occasion, the unfolding of a meaning that, in Haering's terms, "wanted to be".

In order to counter the claim to exclusiveness of those who addressed themselves to what Lutyens called "the High Game", Lethaby proclaimed the true cause of architecture to lie in "High Utility".[19] The most essential contribution that architects of the Other Tradition have made is to redeem the concept of purpose and function from mere use and Functionalism; and Lethaby's proud phrase reasserts the long-lost significance of the powers of transformation and fulfilment upon which the concept of a Practical Art is based.

THE OTHER ORDER

There is one essential characteristic of the kind of architecture that flows from the principles that we have discussed, and that is the extent to which its form is generated and inspired by the particular way of life that called it into being, rather than by the emulation of precedent or the exploration of some abstract *exercice du style*. The gratification of some living purpose must be the grounds of its necessity and the source of its inspiration. It must (as we have just argued) be open to any and every call from whatever quarter it may come.

It is therefore, by definition, not a 'style'; there are no Five Points, no canonical attributes to be codified. The Classical term that matches its aspirations is not *mimesis* but *methexis* — the active power that makes it possible for something to happen. The fact that the desire that brings it into existence is generated from powers that lie far outside the discipline of the art itself exposes each enterprise to the unpredictable. Far from being canonical, its products are more likely to exhibit what Wittgenstein, in a note on Gothic architecture, described as "significant irregularity".[20]

A classic case of the pursuit of an unprecedented invention of form is Scharoun's proposal for 'Music at the centre' in his Berlin Philharmonie. Within the big bowl of the auditorium the acoustic control of reverberation intervals required a very precise modelling of planes. Equally, the pattern of circulation necessary to afford access to seats right around the auditorium demanded a counter-form below (somewhat like walking around a ship in dry-dock), around which the various staircases, bars, cloakrooms and other amenities can be distributed with ease.

Hans Scharoun
Philharmonie,
Berlin, 1956-1963.
Foyer.

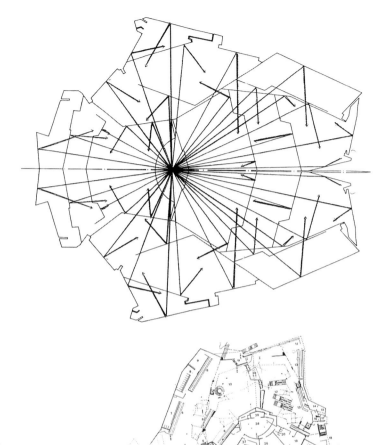

CLOCKWISE
TOP TO BOTTOM:
Hans Scharoun
Philharmonie,
Berlin, 1956–1963.
Acoustic diagram,
entrance level plan,
section and view
of the concert hall.

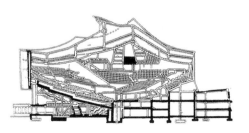

One way to illuminate this point is to recall the statement by Henry-Russell Hitchcock: "each real style of architecture is able to express *certain* functions perfectly.... Only by a loss of perfect integrity can a style succeed in giving the most adequate expression to all the functions."[21] In the same vein Paul Rudolph once claimed that "all problems can never be solved... it is a characteristic of the twentieth century that architects are highly selective in determining which problems they want to solve".[22] This is the plea of the aesthete *par excellence*, the easy way out.

It is, on the contrary, precisely a catholicity of response, an openness to each and every aspect of a desirable form of life for a particular building that we should expect. In Haering's words, "we must understand the special requirements of every task. We cannot set up systems but we have to start again and again and many times right from the beginning."[23] In a similar

Santa Maria della Scala
Siena — transformation and growth in the life of a building.

OPPOSITE:
Hans Scharoun
Darmstadt School Project, 1951.
Model.

vein, Aalto wrote: "there exists one absolute condition for creative work...
in every case one must achieve a simultaneous solution of conflicting
problems".[24] And what is also interesting about this statement is that
it was prefaced by a quotation from Strindberg to demonstrate that the
bringing together of apparently irreconcilable opposites was the condition
of poetry itself — not just a pragmatic compromise.

Nothing can be left out (*pace* Rudolph) because it is too awkward to
be accommodated; each component must have its place and its identity
be given due presence in the whole. This is the vitality of life itself.

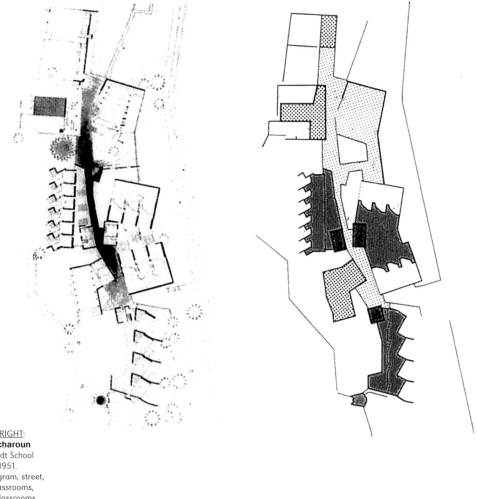

Hans Scharoun
Darmstadt School
Project, 1951.
Plan diagram, street,
junior classrooms,
middle classrooms,
senior classrooms.

For if each part is granted its independence in this way it follows that it will bring with it the scale that is appropriate to its pattern of occupation and use. In proportion to the extent that the specificities of human presence and activity begin to unfold their own identity, the building will begin to attain its true character.

Again it is Scharoun who offers one of the most vivid examples of this differentiation of parts; in his design for a school that he presented at the colloquium on "Man and Space" in Darmstadt in 1951, each of the three groups of classes were designed with unique characteristics of form, orientation to sunlight and relation to open space in order to respond to the age group of the children. Each of these class bases was then distributed together with other shared facilities along a common access route which, far from being a circulation corridor, was more like a village street — a variegated sequence of movement and pause, wide and narrow, opening here onto a courtyard, there onto playing fields. He spoke in terms of "energy" rather than forms to be "found, shaped and filled both by the architect and by the one who uses the building".[25]

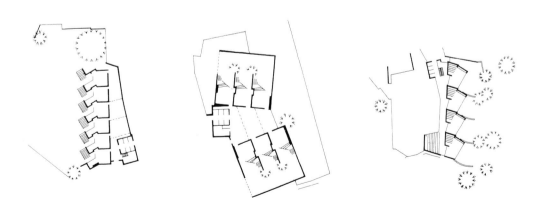

This colloquium was also the occasion upon which the philosopher Martin Heidegger presented his celebrated paper entitled "Building, Dwelling, Thinking".[26] His theme of letting things become themselves, to be what they essentially are and not be "framed" into some kind of other order (*gestell*) is an essential step in Heidegger's existential argument, and it is the very issue upon which Haering challenges Le Corbusier. Scharoun, who was present, admitted to being both familiar with Heidegger's philosophy and greatly sympathetic to it; and it is clear that Haering was similarly very close to Heidegger whose reference in his lecture to the Black Forest Farm is in itself a gloss on all the senses in which Haering's Gut Garkau Farm differs from Le Corbusier's design for the Radiant Farm.

The language of such an architecture will be very different from that of the conventional terms born out of the teaching of the Beaux-Arts schools. Instead of a formal canon grounded in the parameters of 'axis', 'symmetry', '*poché*', 'mosaic' and all the other aids to the graphic presentation of 'paper architecture', we are offered an order based upon the quality of our experience in occupying real buildings — of being outside, or inside, or in the in-between world of the threshold.

This is the quality of habitability in which the emphasis falls not upon the object-like properties of the building itself, but upon the relationship between the building and its occupant. It is a two-way relationship because to every aspect of a building proffered to us we bring a certain sensitivity of response; and it is a relationship that is all the more complex in proportion to the extent that its nature — even its very existence — is not adequately acknowledged and defined. Indeed, the first thing to be said in trying to define this experience is that while it is universal and not at all the privileged sensibility of the aesthete or the learned response of the architect, it suffers from the complete absence of any conscious awareness of it in common parlance. There is no name for this critical sense.

It is very difficult to convey the 'reality' of space in any other terms than actuality. The architect Luigi Moretti made a number of models in which liquid plaster poured into the mould depicts the enclosed space as a positive form, almost to suggest that it is carved. The drawings of Giacometti convey a very different sense of space as a medium charged with directional energies. But this still does not cover the full complexity of our physical experience of space. It seems that it is compounded from a number of interwoven layers of experience. There is the purely physical realm that relates to one's location within a particular portion of space. Secondly, there is a form of body language drawing on the psychological impulses based on empathy — namely the transference into ourselves of mental states corresponding to the structures that surround us, so that we project feelings of trust and support of load into terms of our own bodily sensations. Thirdly, we think

Luigi Moretti
Space model of St Peters, Rome.

in terms of 'being inside' or 'being outside' — in fact all our experience lies at some point in a range running between these two extremes, each of which contains a potential state of panic: claustrophobia and agoraphobia. We all have our own private dispositions towards spatial disquiet — Proust's panic at the high ceiling in his hotel room at Balbec-Plage in contrast to his bedroom at home is a familiar example.

This much at least is a commonly (and clinically) acknowledged fact. But there is also a convincing argument for the presence of a yet further component, psychoanalytical in nature, that lies below the level of our consciousness of physical space but carries with it emotions recalling traumatic experiences from childhood.[27] Melanie Klein is the principal authority and Adrian Stokes the principal expositor of the application to architectural sensibilities of this phenomenon. They argue that this sensibility contains a powerful emotional charge since it is the result of a

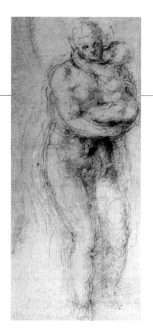

LEFT TO RIGHT:

Michelangelo
Mother and Child.

Giorgio de Chirico
The Child's Brain, 1914.

Hans Scharoun
Philarmonie.
Interior of Concert Hall.

Le Corbusier
Villa at Garches, 1927.

traumatic change experienced in early childhood between two polar positions or modes of experience through which we all pass in infancy. The fact that the word 'position' is chosen to describe a psychoanalytical state alone suggests the relevance of this thesis to spatial experience and therefore to architecture.

The first position is identified as an all-embracing envelopment with the mother, of oneness — a kind of fusion which is the sheltering. Reassurance is complete. This position of envelopment later gives way to the contrary position of exposure — of being outside, vulnerable and required to face an alien world of objects 'out there'. The change from one position to the other is disorienting and it is not difficult to believe the suggestion that this turning inside out of the world of the infant has an effect that is traumatic.

There is a close equivalent to the first position in the architectural experience of being inside a space that is all-embracing, with sensations here drawing most intimately upon the sense of touch and sight and hearing. We are at one with the space that fills the void between us and the surfaces that bound us. The architectural equivalent for the second position lies in the state of being in the open and confronted by the facade of a building.

Suffice it to say that since each of these two psychological positions is charged at the time of our first exposure to them with emotional drama, it would not be surprising to find that some echo of that charge is still latent beneath the surface of all our everyday experience.

We are therefore confronted with the thought that our 'normal' experience of space is shadowed by a parallel narrative spelled out in a body language that we learnt long before words, and which constantly conditions our sense of feeling safe or threatened, exposed or protected in varying gradations of being inside or outside, or hovering on the threshold in-between. And to this language there then becomes added the further range of ambiguous combinations such as an outside-inside (the loggia) or an inside-outside (the atrium).

LEFT TO RIGHT:

P Lequeue
Il est libre, 1799.

Emanuele Rocco
Galleria Umberto 1,
Naples, 1889-1892.

**Aldo van Eyck
& Theo Bosch**
Hubertus House,
Amsterdam, 1976-1980.

But none of this narrative is as simple as it has been presumed to be and this fact alone is worth noting since it may throw some light on the otherwise unexplained force of feeling prompted by the kind of architecture that is felt to be alien. Combinations of these spatial figures form a narrative that is the real art of architecture. And it will be in this medium of charged spatial experience that the masters of the Other Tradition have worked, rather than in the refinement of an object and its 'forms in light'.

What we are therefore offered is a narrative of event and episode where movement, pause and coming to rest are paced in direct response to the activities that the building was built to serve, with something of the precision and the propriety of a rite, yet performed not with the aura and sacred repetition of ritual itself, but the spontaneity of a living pursuit — the unselfconscious participation in a seemingly natural choreography.

By the same token, the breakdown in scale from large to subsidiary forms will be made not so much by stressing the mode of structural assembly (as, for instance, in Kahn's claim that there is enough decoration in the marks of a building's construction), nor by the game of proportional composition on planar surfaces (as in Le Corbusier's *tracés régulateurs*), but rather by the elements that respond to human presence and touch (a rubbing-strake, a dado, a handrail, built-in furniture and fittings), the intimate language of inhabitation.

We are therefore concerned with a way of working that sees a building not as an object to be contemplated from without but to be entered, experienced within, used. Goethe, whose unravelling of the origins of the amphitheatre have been cited as an example of the way in which architecture is generated from the desire to enjoy a spectacle, defined that process as analogous to the processes of nature working "from inside out" ("*von innen hinaus*"). So far so good, for that is precisely the opposite procedure from that which starts out with a set of forms into which the content will be shoe-horned with varying degrees of fluke, compromise and mismatch. But it is an analogy with a process, not with a set of forms. In this sense it is important to understand that when, for instance, Alvar Aalto (in discussing the advantages and limitations of standards for mass-production) draws an analogy to the variations within a type to be found in plant forms, he is not, as is too often suggested, proposing the adoption of particular organic shapes. Rather, he is pointing, like Cuvier and D'Arcy Wentworth Thompson, to an enormously rich play between family type and variant. Employment of the term 'organic' in this context is not intended as a literal analogy to the forms of nature nor to point to some hypothetical freedom of form, but to a process that makes possible a greater precision of form.

Cuvier's assertion that from one bone he could reconstruct the entire anatomy of an animal, is based upon his claim that "every organised being forms a whole, a unique and closed system, whose parts mutually correspond. None of its parts can change without the others also changing; and consequently each of them taken separately, indicates and determines all the others."[28] To an architect, that very phraseology carries a ringing echo of the famous assertion by Alberti of the *concinnitas* of Classical form which he described as "that reasoned harmony of all parts within a body such that nothing can be added, taken away or altered but for the worse".[29] It has recently been argued very convincingly that what Alberti meant by *concinnitas* was not simply a Platonic geometrical formula for modular integrity but a concept that refers to Aristotle's "functional unity of all the parts".[30] The parallel between the claims of Alberti and Cuvier is therefore not superficial; rather it helps to sustain in a wider meaning the integrative power of the fundamental theme of *telos*. The poet, Paul Valéry, condenses this analogy with classic precision in his Socratic dialogue *Eupalinos or the Architect* when he points to:

the almost miraculous conformity of an object with the function that it must fulfil. The perfection of this aptitude excites in our souls the feeling of a relationship between the beautiful and the necessary; and the final ease or simplicity of the result, compared with the intricacy of the problem, fills us with an indescribable enthusiasm.... Nothing but what is of strict utility finds a place in such happy fabrications: they no longer contain anything not solely deduced from the exigencies of the desired effect.

This Classical commitment to the fulfilment of purpose is also reflected in two of the great Romantic formulations of the nineteenth century. First the passage from the *Biographia Literaria* of Samuel Taylor Coleridge:

The form is mechanic when on any given material we impose a pre-determined form, not necessarily arising out of the properties of the material, as when to a mass of wet clay we give whatever shape we wish it to retain when hardened. The organic form, on the other hand, is innate; it shapes as it develops itself from within, and the fullness of its development is one and the same with the perfection of its outward form. Such is the life, such is the form. Nature, the primogenital artist, inexhaustible in diverse powers, is equally inexhaustible in forms.

Secondly, there is the great purple passage by John Ruskin in which he praises the unlimited capacity of Gothic architecture to respond to all and every demand uninhibited by any preordained set of rules:

LEFT TO RIGHT:

William Butterfield
All Saints, Margaret Street, 1850-1859.

Norman Shaw
Leys Wood, 1868.

Henry Hobson Richardson
Trinity Church, Boston, 1872-1877.

LS Buffington
House in Minneapolis, 1888.

Gothic is not only the best but the only rational architecture, as being that which can fit itself most easily to all services, vulgar or noble. Undefined in its slope of roof, height of shaft, breadth of arch, or disposition of ground plan, it can shrink into a turret, expand into a hall, coil into a staircase or spring into a spire, with undegraded grace and unexhausted energy; and whenever it finds occasion for change in its form or purpose, it submits to it without the slightest sense of loss either to its unity or majesty — subtle and flexible like a fiery serpent, but ever attentive to the voice of its charmer. And it is one of the virtues of the Gothic builders that they never suffered ideas of outside symmetries and consistencies to interfere with the real use and value of what they did. If they wanted a window, they opened one; a room, they added one; a buttress, they built one.[31]

To quote this famous passage is to be reminded that the origins of this Other Tradition lie in that extraordinary initiative in the history of British architecture that is known as the English Free School: an initiative that, born and nurtured in the work of William Butterfield, George Edmund Street, Alfred Waterhouse, Norman Shaw, Charles Rennie Mackintosh, Philip Webb and WR Lethaby gained fresh blood in the United States through the inventions of Henry Hobson Richardson and Frank Lloyd Wright

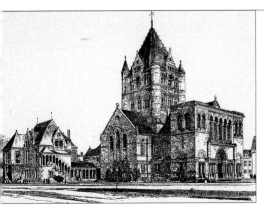 

before returning to inspire the very members of the Resistance of whom I write. For it was in Germany that the rather erratic theoretical basis deriving from Pugin, Ruskin, Morris and Lethaby was given a firmer intellectual and technical structure; above all by Hermann Muthesius and the Viennese Adolf Loos who both acknowledged the English precedent. It is the one moment in British architectural history that made an original contribution to the course of architecture on an international scale; and, if the claims of Muthesius are taken into account, it is the true theoretical foundation of the Modern Movement. The way in which this message was transmitted is well illustrated in the plates of Muthesius' *Das Englische Haus* and FR Vogel's *Das Americanisch Haus*, 1908–1910.

Even here we have to beware of the denigration of the aesthetes whose sole criteria are stylistic and who, in their bafflement at the bewildering range of forms thrown up by what Street called "the need to accommodate our architecture to every want of this nineteenth and most exigent of centuries", have sought to marginalise it as 'picturesque'. Neither in motivation nor in design method is this remotely the case.

Charles Rennie Mackintosh
Glasgow School of Art, 1896–1909.

It is also a concern of this tradition that it should widen the ends to be served every bit as much as to widen the means. A building will not be seen as an isolated object. Responses to the physical context of contour and neighbour, orientation and climate should inflect the form and disposition of every element in a deeply purposeful way: every house built by Scharoun is a fresh exploration of the endless resources of habitat. But equally, the sense of history, of *genius loci*, informs and suffuses the design with a poetic sensibility that is totally absent in the Cartesian abstractions of the International Style.

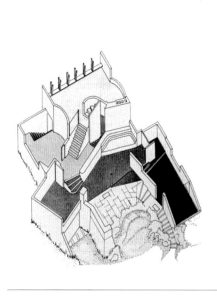

Such embeddedness carries a double import. In the first place it is clear proof that the inspirations of design did spring from the desire for a certain way of living. The second point is made by the challenging statement of Aalto: "... what matters is not what a building looks like when it is first built but what it is like thirty years later". No other form of art is so brutally put to the test over the question of whether or not it works. It may be that a building is demolished because the purposes that called it into being in the first place have themselves become obsolete, but more often than not, demolition is the price paid by a building that never fulfilled its true calling in the first place, never drew its inspiration from life but played instead a silly game with itself.

These are all themes that resist categorisation or formulae: the only way to let them speak is therefore by exemplification and comparative case studies in which a work of the Resistance is compared with an exemplar of orthodox practice.

LEFT TO RIGHT:
Hans Scharoun
Moll House,
Berlin, 1936.

NOTES——CHAPTER FOUR

1 Conversation with the author, 1959.

2 Le Corbusier, *When the Cathedrals were White*, FE Hyslop trans., London: Routledge & Kegan Paul Ltd, 1948, p. 30.

3 Haering, Hugo, "Approaches to Architectural Form", *Die Form*, 1925/1.

4 Le Corbusier, "Vers une Architecture", from the collection *de L'Esprit Nouveau*, Paris: Crés, 1923.

5 Schildt, Goran, *Alvar Aalto: The Decisive Years*, New York: Rizzoli, 1986, p. 226.

6 Recounted in *Oppositions*, no. 4, 1974.

7 Attributed to Villiers de l'Isle Adam.

8 It has to be conceded that this revolutionary model was much in the air at that time and many attempts were made by artist groups — De Stijl, Constructivist, Ma, Vesch, etc., to set up an "international organisation of creative persons of revolutionary outlook".

9 This event is described in some detail in Benedict Zucchi's *Giancarlo de Carlo*, Oxford: Butterworth, 1992.

10 *Forum*, no. 1, 1962.

11 Willetts, John, *The New Objectivity*, London: Thames and Hudson, 1978.

12 Willetts, *The New Objectivity*.

13 See Stanford Anderson's introduction to Hermann Muthesius' *Style-Architecture and Building-Art*, Los Angeles: Getty Centre Publications, 1994.

14 Even Pevsner's "obvious" example is highly vulnerable. There are "garden-sheds" in Kyoto that are to be numbered among the purest examples of architecture in the world and there are glaringly obvious episodes in St Paul's Cathedral (notably the structure of the crossing) that are patently inept as building.

15 Wittgenstein, Ludwig, *Philosophical Investigations*, Oxford: Blackwell, 1953.

16 Wittgenstein, *Philosophical Investigations*, 1: 66.
17 Wittgenstein, *Philosophical Investigations*, 1: 67.
18 Haering, Hugo, "Kunst-und strukturprobleme des bauens", *Zentralblatt der Bauverwaltung Heft 29*, 15 July 1931.
19 Lethaby, WR, *Form in Civilization*, Oxford: Oxford University Press, 1922, p. 9.
20 Wittgenstein, Ludwig, *Culture and Value*, Oxford: Blackwell, 1980, p. 34.
21 Hitchcock, HR, *Modern Architecture, Romanticism and Reintegration*, New York: Payson and Clark Ltd., 1929, p. 216.
22 Rudolph, Paul, *Perspecta*, no. 7, p. 41.
23 Haering, Hugo in conversation with Eiermann et al, 1952, *Baukunst und Werkform*, no. 5, 1952.
24 Aalto, Alvar, "Art and Technology", 1955, in *Sketches*, Cambridge, MA: MIT Press, 1978.
25 Staber, Margit, "Hans Scharoun: A Contribution to Organic Building", in *Zodiac*, no. 10.
26 English translation published in Martin Heidegger, *Poetry, Language, Thought*, New York: Harper & Row, 1975. This book contains the much more important essay entitled "The Origin of the Work of Art".
27 This topic is discussed at greater length in "The Natural Imagination", ch. 1 of my book *Architectural Reflections*, Oxford: Butterworth, 1992.
28 Quoted in Caroline van Eck, *Organicism in Nineteenth-Century Architecture*, Amsterdam: Architecture and Natura Press, p. 217.
29 Alberti, LB, *Ten Books of Architecture*.
30 Van Eck, *Organicism*.
31 Ruskin, John, "The Nature of Gothic", ch. 6 of *The Stones of Venice*, vol. 2, published separately in 1853.

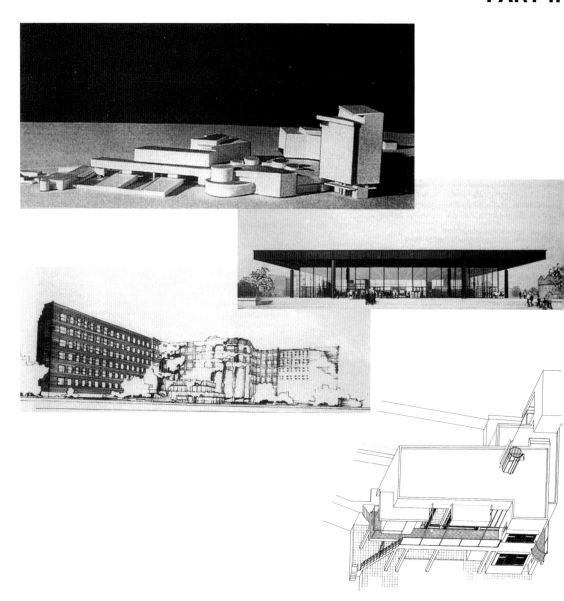

OUR CASE STUDIES

The meaning lies in the use.

LUDWIG WITTGENSTEIN

In order to understand the characteristic features of any object it is helpful to compare it with a different example of the same species. The French verb *accuser* covers both the sense in which one brings a charge against someone (contrast Zola's "*J'accuse*") and the process of sharpening the focus upon whatever is under inspection. In this way one proposition becomes a critique of the other by the demonstration of differences. This is particularly so in the case of buildings in which those differences manifest themselves at every level of decision — form, function and technology.

In order, therefore, to understand what the real differences in practice between the orthodox and the Other Traditions are we will explore a number of such comparisons. In all cases the architects are of high repute. What is at issue is the extent to which the forms they have invented drew their inspiration from the true purposes which the building was required to serve, or from some less relevant tactic, pursued for its own sake.

I have found the most rewarding examples of such comparisons in the work of Aalto whose priority and pre-eminence among the architects of the Resistance I noted in the prologue to this book. His practice has been a touchstone for this point of view right from the start and his own extensive writings confirm the point of view that is implicit in his buildings. It would, however, be a gross distortion of my argument to limit its exemplification to one architect. I therefore include not only Scharoun but also one case study of two works which both take, as their point of departure, Le Corbusier's Five Points — the house at Roquebrune of Eileen Gray and its close contemporary, the house at Le Pradet for Mme de Mandrot by Le Corbusier. Here again there is substantial written evidence of the architects' intentions in both cases.

CASE 1: THE TOWN HALL

The most obvious examples for comparative study are presented by the various solutions offered in an architectural competition where the same set of requirements are addressed by a number of architects, and our first case is therefore just such a competition that took place for the Town Hall at Marl in Germany.

The ends to be served by a town hall are principally two. The pattern of operations of a number of separate administrative departments require an efficient distribution of front of house and behind the scenes working space. Secondly, in its role as the centre of a community's authority and public services, a town hall has to project an image that establishes a clear entity and an appropriately welcoming invitation to visitors.

At the time of the competition, 1958, the Modernist orthodoxy was dominated by two buildings of outstanding authority in formal terms — the Unité d'Habitation of Le Corbusier and the Seagram Building of Mies van der Rohe. One became the archetype for mass housing and the other for offices and administrative buildings; one the prototypical demonstration of mass production in concrete elements, the other in steel and glass. Together they came to exercise over the minds of architects during a period of world-wide post-war reconstruction, the authority of instant solutions. The revolution had truly become, in Aalto's phrase, "a Dictatorship".

Arne Jacobsen
Marl Town Hall
Competition, 1950.
Model.

This fact is clearly demonstrated in the design submissions. Scheme after scheme offered minor variants upon the theme of the Miesian multi-storey curtain wall cubic block combined with lower cubes disposed on a rectangular grid. Among these, the winning scheme by Bakema won the prize for its technical enterprise by introducing a novel form of suspension structure; but the relevance to the Town Hall of this piece of derring-do remains unexplained.

In none of these projects is there any departure from the orthogonal grid, either in plan or elevation or surface grain. The only variation between one cube and another lies in their size, while their distribution is determined by a system of corridor planning which, in some cases, runs the entire length of the site. As to site planning, there is no evidence of any sensitivity to the contextual differentiation between the noisy road frontage to the south and the existing park to the north. Insofar as identity or representational form is a concern, none of these proposals could be taken to be more than commercial office buildings: they belong strictly to the territory that Christian Norberg-Schulz aptly dismissed as "a space without secrets".

However, two projects dramatically rejected these predetermined criteria, and both of them were produced by members of the Resistance to whom I have made frequent reference — Hans Scharoun and Alvar Aalto.

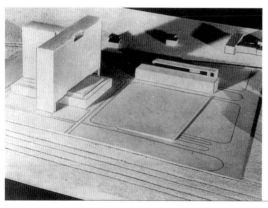

The first thing to notice about these two designs is that they are not at all what Hitchcock and his fellow historians would have them be — exercises in Expressionism whose primary objective was to be different: for as we shall see there is, between these two projects, a fundamental similarity which is of great significance. In hierarchy, contextual inflection and topology, this conformity is not a stylistic fluke but derives from precisely the factors of origin that were discussed in Chapter Four.

Scharoun opens his project report with the statement that the city is the "mirror of its social structure, it makes visible the forces that keep its life going.... Its purposes and way of working should find a way of being expressed — a way that makes sense to the community too."

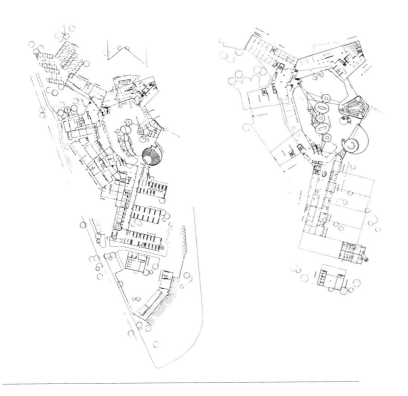

OPPOSITE LEFT:

F Kramer
Marl Town Hall
Competition, 1950.
Model.

OPPOSITE RIGHT,
LEFT AND RIGHT:

Hans Scharoun
Marl Town Hall
Competition, 1950.
Model, ground floor
plan and upper floor
plan.

The way he sets about it is to give every part of the programme its own identity. Thus, each of the five departments is a separate element clustered in a radiating form like the thumb and fingers of a hand around the palm — which here corresponds to the main public reception hall. The sixth element enclosing the Central Hall is the Assembly Room and Debating Chamber complex. The closed mass of these elements, whose cylindrical form signals to the main road their symbolic presence, acts as a protective screen against the noise of the main street. Scharoun calls this Central Hall space "a year-round environmentally controlled space within which, unlike the conventional Town Hall which tends to frighten its citizens, an atmosphere of human invitation can be developed". The highest level of the complex is crowned with a cafeteria overlooking the whole town and the lowest level is a public beer cellar. There is easy access to this centre, both by vehicle or by foot, from the park. Leading out of the Central Hall is the quieter information centre offering a number of educational facilities he likens to an Open University. This whole interpretation of the brief recalls the famous ecstatic thesis put forward after the First World War by Bruno Taut in his book *Die Stadtkrone* (*The Crown of the City*). This was an evocative reminder of the way in which historically, in both Eastern and Western cultures, the spirit of the town or city was celebrated as the dominant iconographic presence at its centre. Scharoun's report includes the suggestion that the phrase "We build a city" should be inscribed on a banner visible from afar, as it is important for everyone to understand the structure of the city — "people who do not build, die".

What is extraordinary about this project is the way in which the explosive but bewildering dynamics of his early Expressionist days have been brought to the service of a very complex and deeply responsible social contract, and in doing so have brought to bear, in their own way, a discipline as controlled as it is unpredictable. And what it is controlling is the ambition to give each element of the whole complex the individual form that fulfils its pattern of activities and, at the same time, proudly disports its own identity. In doing so Scharoun provided a brilliant exposition of Hugo Haering's definition of Natural Form: "... the organization of many distinct parts in space so that life can unfold, fulfilling all its goals both in terms of the simple part and of the integrated whole".[1]

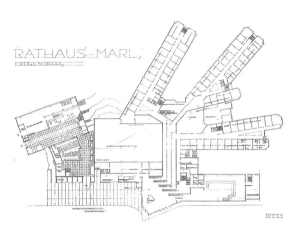

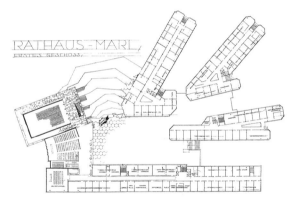

TOP TO BOTTOM:
Alvar Aalto
Marl Town Hall
Competition, 1950.
Lower floor plan, upper
floor plan and model,
1958.

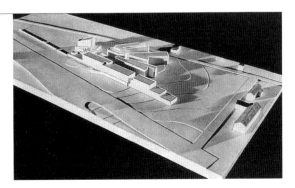

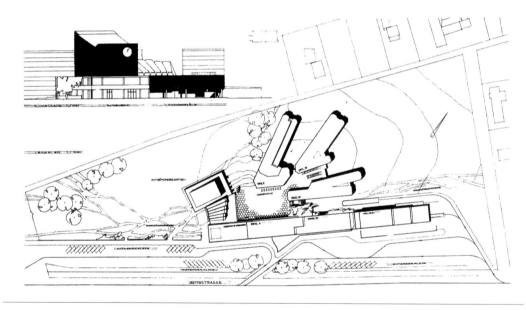

Alvar Aalto
Marl Town Hall
Competiton, 1950.
Roof plan and elevation.

Aalto's scheme is also focused upon a raised courtyard solidly screened from traffic on the main road to the south but opening into the neighbouring park by gently descending stepped contours. The dominant element here is the massive auditorium which is oriented towards the centre of the town. The Mayor and councillors' rooms are sited below this with their own discrete entrance. The administrative offices then fan out from this focal point like the fingers of a hand (and here, the analogy to Scharoun's scheme is striking). The superstructure of each of the four wings is freestanding so that not only does each have its own scale and identity, but also permits glimpses between each out into the park. A further analogy to the form of an Italian hill-town with its forum created by a cluster of protective structures, is reinforced by the use of broad surfaces of brick. At the entrance level the Central Registry Office reflects the courtyard above and, from this common information point, access is directly presented to the information counter of all five departments. In this way the pattern of activity of visitors to the building is made doubly intelligible by conforming to the pattern of expectations set up by the form of the superstructure. Aalto's own account of the order of the building describes it as "an attempt to resolve what is basically a representational problem by means of a special form of organisation", and adds:

> a municipal government building is not just an ordinary office block; the wide range of different functions of varying importance ought to be legible from the outside without attempting to strive for geometrical monumentality. The building ought to be closely integrated with the beautiful park to become a pleasurably accessible forum for all the people of the town.

What is clear about both these projects is that the origin and inspiration of their form lies in a sustained appreciation of their civic purposes, representational as much as operational; a sensitive response to the character of the site; and the invention of an organic order supple enough to respond to the many differentiated demands in its pattern of use but articulate enough in embodying those characteristics to produce a form that is vivid and intelligible.

Paradoxically, the further the project pursues the difference in patterns of operation, the more it takes on a narrative quality in which character and hierarchy blossom into a form of rhetoric — only this time it is not the rhetoric of conventional symbols and familiar forms. The facts become poetry. What is even further convincing is that the underlying figure of the outspread hand with elements fanning out from a centre was derived by each architect quite independently of the other. Both, it seems, had elicited this form as the hidden truth, the *aletheia*, at the heart of the brief. And so it is that these two projects differ from their rivals not only by their evocative and authentic imagery, but also by their common divination of an inner truth — use, form and symbol combining to become one thing, not an office block but the city crown.

**Alvar and Elissa Aalto
and J-J Baruël**
Art Museum in Aalborg,
1958-1973.
Model and exterior.

CASE 2: THE ART GALLERY

As a building type, the art gallery presents an ideal focus for the comparative study of a form of building whose task may be specified fairly precisely, and its resolution demonstrated by examination above all of interior spaces. For the display of works of art the control of light sources is now a subject of familiar performance criteria (such as the avoidance of reflections, glare and fall-off of light levels) and value judgements (such as the balance of natural and artificial light sources). Secondly, as a public institution it will have a responsibility to declare its identity by its external presence.

On the evidence of many recently designed art galleries, it is clear that this building type is a true test of the architect's understanding of the difference between a work of Fine Art and a work of Practical Art — all too many architects assume that they are required to design the building itself as a work of art rather than a building to house works of art. The two conditions are not just different, they are completely opposed.

The works selected for purpose of comparison are the National Gallery in Berlin by Mies van der Rohe, 1962–1968, and the North Jutland Art Museum by Alvar and Aino Aalto in association with Jean-Jacques Baruël, 1958–1972, at Aalborg in northern Denmark.

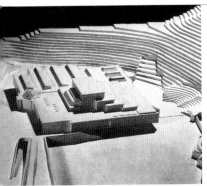

Aalto said that "light is to the art gallery what acoustics are to the concert hall", and at Aalborg he has designed in section so as to introduce daylight into galleries in a number of different ways and thus meeting the different requirements of painting and sculpture. It is evidently a public building, with great presence in the landscape, and an elegant facade clad in Carrara marble. Cars are conducted away from invading the scene since access is provided by a ramp straight from the road and under the building to a lower level car park, restaurant and garden. This calmly controlled manipulation of the fall in the site is elaborated at the lower level by carving the contours into a sculpture court at one side, an amphitheatre for outdoor performance of various kinds in the centre, and a park screened by trees to the right.

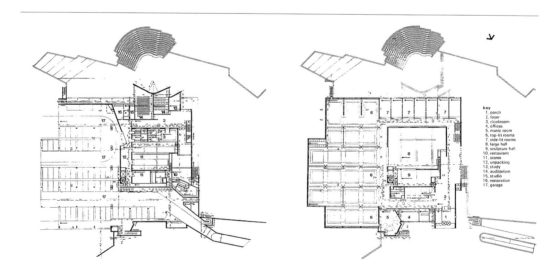

key
1. porch
2. foyer
3. cloakroom
4. offices
5. music room
6. top-lit rooms
7. side-lit rooms
8. large hall
9. sculpture hall
10. restaurant
11. stores
12. unpacking
13. study
14. auditorium
15. studio
16. restoration
17. garage

The upper level plan has a very straightforward disposition of spaces in the form of a central exhibition gallery for temporary exhibitions, and a series of permanent exhibition rooms of different sizes arranged around it in an L-shape on two sides. The rooms are all characterised by an extraordinary modelling of the ceiling and its rooflights, thereby producing an overhead experience analogous to clouds that keep changing and distributing light from the sky in many different ways.

LEFT TO RIGHT:
**Alvar and Elissa Aalto
and J-J Baruël**
Art Museum in Aalborg,
1958–1973.
Lower floor plan,
upper floor plan
and permanent
collection gallery.

Le Corbusier once declared famously that "the plan is the generator": in this case you could better say "the ceiling is the generator". The temporary exhibition hall is preponderantly lit by a large conventional north light clerestory window. However, Aalto wanted to introduce some sunlight into the space in one way or another: "We have designed the geometry of the louvres very carefully but we don't want the building to make you feel that you are in an aquarium." His original idea was that south-facing clerestory windows would receive sunlight by reflection up from trays of water so that the sunlight could thus enter indirectly onto the underside of the main ceiling. It would furthermore have the vitality of the shimmering play of light that is one of the joys of sailing when sunlight reflects up from water onto the bulkhead of a boat. Eventually, he used white marble slabs instead of water, but the quality of reflection is retained. The light is then reflected down off a curvilinear roof section that Aalto further articulates by cutting it away from one wall face. Behind this central gallery a small sculpture gallery is lit by vertical or slightly skewed funnel skylights.

LEFT AND OPPOSITE:
Alvar and Elissa Aalto and J-J Baruël
Art Museum in Aalborg 1958–1973.
Temporary exhibition gallery and cross-sections.

In the flanking galleries assigned to the permanent collections, a very different daylight is introduced through monitors which reflect light down on either side of a suspended access-way, which serves the additional purpose of allowing manual adjustment to the array of artificial lights. Here, light is manipulated on a different scale and the axis of the light source is asymmetrically arranged so that the quality of light is always changing throughout the day. By these subtle and inventive variations the inimitable qualities of natural light — its colour, and sensitive shifts in value — are manipulated not only to show the works of art to maximum advantage but also to create an ambience that will stimulate and sustain the concentration of the visitor.

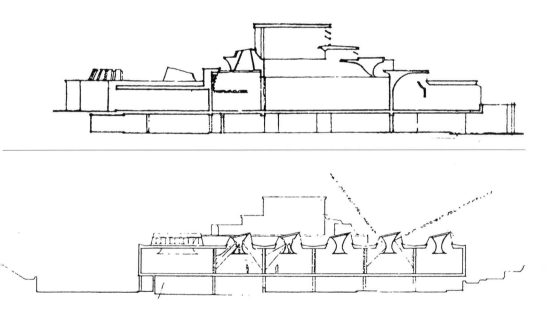

In Mies van der Rohe's National Gallery in Berlin, we have a very different response to the requirements which in all essentials are the same — a gallery for the temporary exhibition of works on loan and a home for the permanent collection. Here, the temporary exhibition gallery is a large glass-walled space at an upper level and the permanent collection is placed on a separate level below. Clearly, the context of central Berlin is very different from Aalborg and here we have something which is, at first, quite manifestly a rhetorical urban statement. It is primarily a technical statement about a steel structure — but is presented as a glass temple on a broad 'acropolis', thus proclaiming the National Gallery's monumental status.

OPPOSITE
TOP TO BOTTOM:
Mies van der Rohe
National Gallery, Berlin
1962–1967.
Stair down
into basement,
permanent collection
in basement, temporary
exhibition gallery and
ground floor plan.

CLOCKWISE
TOP TO BOTTOM:
Mies van der Rohe
National Gallery, Berlin,
1962–1967.
Site model, approach
to the Acropolis and
entrance.

In the interior, the manipulation of daylight is very different from that at Aalborg. Instead of being filtered into the building from clerestories and roof lights and thereby directed from above onto the surface of the works to be viewed, it is relegated to the perimeter. There, by the use of huge transparent glass wall panels, it becomes charged into an unmediated source of glare. The result is that the exhibits can be viewed as virtually unlit objects silhouetted against a dazzling wall of light to the extent that all subtle variations in colour, tonal value and texture are destroyed. This, quite simply, flouts the primary purpose for which the building was commissioned.

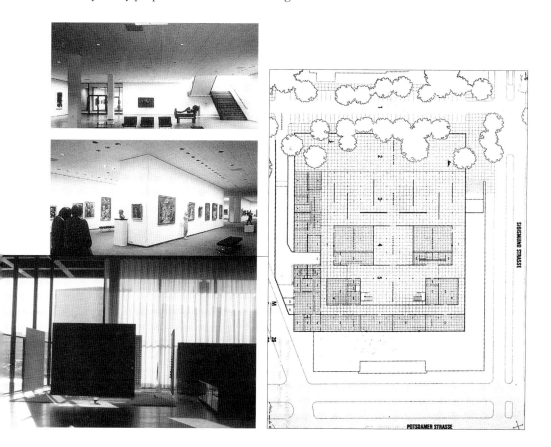

In the basement, the permanent collection takes the form of an underworld of corridors and artificial lighting. It is a featureless warren offering no distinction to the works, nor stimulation to the viewer. There is some daylight at the far end, where the visitors may gratefully wander out and find themselves in a pleasant little walled courtyard. But then a surprise unfolds. For this courtyard permits a view of the glass temple floating above, and in so doing, completely undermines the initial reading of the building as a temple sitting on a massive podium. What has happened to the acropolis? Sadly it has become completely undermined; and so has the rhetoric.

The Berlin National Gallery is a late (last) work and Mies had perhaps but one thought in mind — in the city of his beloved Schinkel to make his own response to the temple of his master, the Altes Museum. He wanted to create a temple of his own — a steel temple. Paul Rudolph once wrote: "Mies makes wonderful buildings only because he ignores many aspects of a building."[2] In this case what he ignored was, alas, the very "end other than itself" that a gallery has to serve — the presentation and celebration of works of art.

In Berlin the driving force was a preoccupation with the technology of steel construction and the extent to which, through *mimesis*, it could evoke the form of the Classical temple. Set against the true purposes for which the building was commissioned, the irrelevance and internal contradictions, latent in such preoccupations, are brutally revealed.

In Aalborg, form, siting and detail all grew and took their inspiration from the essence of the end to be served through *methexis* and a poetic manipulation of the inherent possibilities of the site. Ironically, too, the whole composition echoes the elements of a Greek temple site in a far more apposite way than the acropolis of Mies.

LEFT TO RIGHT:
Mies van der Rohe
National Gallery, Berlin, 1962–1967.
Permanent collection in basement, basement courtyard and rear elevation.

CASE 3: THE STUDENT HALL OF RESIDENCE

It is germane to our general thesis that in this case the architects of the two buildings personify, in the case of Gropius, CIAM orthodoxy and, in the case of Aalto, the Resistance. The buildings are two student halls of residence built in the same city, Boston, in 1949: the Harvard Graduate Center by Walter Gropius and Baker House at MIT by Alvar and Aino Aalto.

As a building type, the hall of residence demands above all a fine balance between, on the one hand, the shared facilities, with their invitation to communal occasion and places of meeting and, on the other hand, the vital need to ensure the privacy of the individual.

In specific terms, the requirements for Harvard and MIT were similar — accommodation for students in single and shared rooms and provision of certain facilities such as dining and common rooms. In both cases there were constraints of strict economy. Finally, both buildings were the occasion for exploration with students as studio projects where Gropius was head of the department at Harvard and Aalto a visiting professor at MIT.

There all similarity ends. Gropius' approach and the priority of values that he brought to the theme are reflected in the way he set it out as a studio project for his students. His adherence to a grindingly pragmatic brief culled from three sets of university estate sources, is presented to the students as a down to earth introduction to the 'real world of practice'. No incentive was given to challenge the values of that world of accountancy; economy (the *Existenzminimum* once more) appears to be the sole value. Thus the ratio of single to double rooms is determined in favour of the latter on economic grounds without any attempt to seek student preference through survey: certainly there is no case here of participation with the future inhabitants. And the genial suggestion that some shared lounges might be introduced was not exactly encouraged by the suggestion that a location for them might be sought "in the basement"! It concludes:

The final solution to the problem must therefore be based on finding a balance between the relatively rigid requirements of economy and construction and the less definable requirements which, when met, provide a stimulating environment for education.

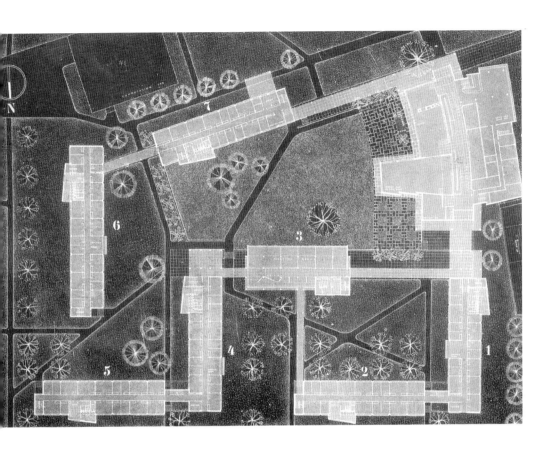

**Walter Gropius
and The Architects' Collaborative**
Harvard Graduate Center, 1949.
Site plan.

In the case of "the less definable requirements" no attempt at all was made to define them. The simulation of real practice in an office is here confined to the rag-bag of unrelated pragmatic fall-out rather than the creative process of formulating and reformulating priorities in some sort of dialogue with client and inhabitant. No advantage was taken of the possibility of opening up unpredictable possibilities through the participation of a range of students.

This approach confirms only too well the devastating account of Gropius' teaching methods at both the Bauhaus and at Harvard, presented by Klaus Herdeg in his book *The Decorated Diagram*.[3] In that book, Herdeg analysed, at great length, the kind of work that emerged from what he recalled "this language of pseudoscientific pragmatism". It is also saddening to see that when at last Gropius did teach architecture (which he had done at the Bauhaus) it was to adopt the most deadening of practices of Hannes Meyer whom he professed to deplore.

The design procedure inculcated into the students was virtually the opposite of what we have described as the Beaux-Arts method; and equally meretricious. Instead of imagination, historical reference, formal

composition, and virtuoso graphic representation, we are offered a bubble-diagram of functional zones given visual excitement by an overlay of texture or pattern of the kind 'explored' in a first year Bauhaus Basic Design course. Visual cues defy resolution because they do not fuse or reinforce each other to establish an overall meaning; certainly any reference to historic precedent was ruled out (history was not on the required syllabus). The end product of this procedure is the haphazard record of random events (programme, legal and financial restrictions, choice of materials, expressive elements) rather than a meaningful order answering to an intelligible theme. A comparison between the procedure for student projects in the Bauhaus method and the Beaux-Arts method offers a perfect mirroring of the division created by the concepts of Functionalism and 'art for art's sake' — disasters both.

The buildings that were finally produced to the design of Gropius and his associates bear the mark of the impoverished ethos that engendered them. A handful of 'Harvard boxes' are disposed in an arrangement whose grouping or isolation, interconnection or detachment, variety in number of floors, orientation of balconies, and linkage to or separation from the Dining Hall complex all fail to respond to any perceptible integrative order.

OPPOSITE AND RIGHT:
**Walter Gropius and
The Architects'
Collaborative**
Harvard Graduate
Center, 1949.
Aerial view, typical block
and typical double-
room.

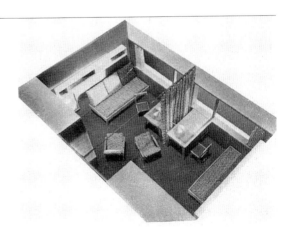

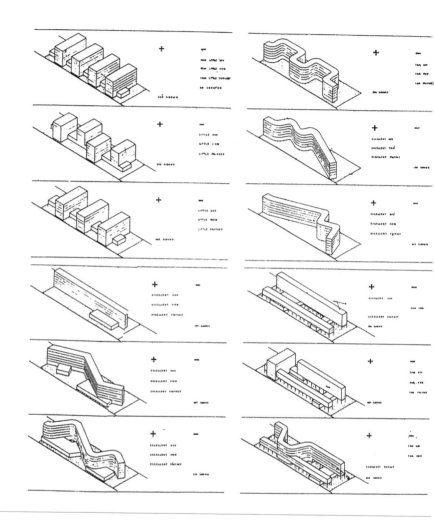

TOP AND BOTTOM:
Alvar and Aino Aalto
Baker House, MIT,
1947–1948.
Alternative plan forms
One and Two.

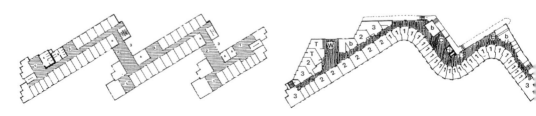

By contrast we see that Aalto, fully accepting the constraint of economy, nevertheless engages it as part of a complex equation that gives equal value to four other parameters: privacy, views of the Charles River, sunlight to each room, and number of rooms included. And so, within the limits of frontage determined by the site, a dozen alternative layouts are produced and compared on the basis of a score card marking each of the four parameters. Note that, at the very least, this approach encourages the accountants to see that there are other values than money. Note also that it dismisses once and for all the blind spot of the style-minders of the orthodoxy who, at that time, denigrated the building as an example of "eccentric Expressionism" (Hitchcock) or "the irrational" (Giedion); no design process could be more deeply ordered or rational than that pursued by Aalto for this building.

Clearly, his preferred method for facing the maximum number of rooms towards the river was to increase the linear run of that frontage by inflecting it into double curvature; and this solution (which was retained in the final form) offered the possibility of holding the whole of the north side of the building together with a monumental double staircase starting from a single controlled point at the entry (which was a requirement of the brief). In this way he achieved all of the characteristics that he sought for the private rooms — view, privacy and sunlight — and, from the cascading staircase with its tributary lounges, all of the points of contact and meeting that are necessary to the life and identity of a community. The project was at risk for some time because it did not contain quite enough rooms. It was, however, saved by a proposal (which Aalto credited to Aino) to add a 'bustle' of rooms facing southwest to the river at the western extremity of the frontage.

Before this resolution of the problem was proposed, he had considered a completely alternative scheme and his manner of doing so offers us a clear indication of his inclusive but open-minded thinking. It was a solution that entailed the loss of the grand staircase and all that it provided as a focus of meeting and exchange; and so he compensated for this by multiplying the number of lounges at the end and 'bridge' locations between the wings of the building. It is also clear that, as he stated in a letter to the Dean, he preferred to start from scratch rather than compromise the unitary nature of the original proposal; in other words, he was prepared to abandon the wonderful double-curvature if it did not serve its purpose.

Alvar and Aino Aalto
Baker House, MIT,
1947–1948.
River (south) elevation
and north elevation
frontage (model).

It was to the Dean at MIT, John Burchard, that Aalto addressed a famous telegram that has the Nelson touch of a battle-order run up the main mast: "the enemy number one today is modern formalism... true architecture, the real thing, is only where man stands at the centre". That claim could only carry meaning by being put to the test in some way and inevitably it recalls the pronouncement of Aalto that we have already quoted: "It is not what a building looks like on the opening day but what it is like thirty years later that counts." It is revealing that not one of the other Masters of CIAM had either concerned themselves with such a criterion or dared to offer such a hostage to fortune. The fact is that a feedback review of any building is an extremely rare phenomenon. In the case of Baker House, however, we have precisely that — an extended review carried out by two of the students 30 years after the opening of the building.[4] The findings of that review are indeed quite remarkable. It explored:

> the effectiveness of Aalto's simultaneous concerns for the particular needs of the individual inhabitant and for the support necessary to develop a group living experience.... If the design was that of a Master the result has been active participation.

Three factors in particular were identified as contributory to what is meant here by "active participation" and to the sustained popularity of the building among successive generations of residents. Firstly, the variations in shape and size of the individual rooms stimulated a rich framework for improvised participation by the inhabitants. The rooms ranged from one to three occupants and the diversity of their shape is reflected in the way the students labelled them as "coffins, pies and couches". The review states:

> the result is something like a local folk art of room building.... There is a kind of population of room constructions which moves through the building with their owners, is passed on to later users, or, upon graduation, is sold to newcomers with compatible rooms. (A construction designed for a 'coffin', for example, may not fit a 'pie' or 'couch'.)

As to the shared elements, it was made clear that three lounges on each floor — dining hall, recreation area and the monumental stairway — created a sense of place and community that was unique for the whole MIT campus:

> The central stair provides easy communication between floors and may contribute to room assignment priorities. Together with the floor lounges, it provides a tree of communication, meeting and circulation spaces along the north side of the building as a complement to the private and semi-private rooms along the south face.

The review particularly underlined the importance of the shared lounges by recording that whereas, during the 1960s, the authorities substituted student rooms for the central lounges (in order to increase student accommodation and thereby reduce the rent), the Student House Committee were at the time of the review demanding reversion to the original layout in spite of the increase in rent that would ensue. Aalto, evidently, had got it right in the beginning.

A further gloss upon the difference between Gropius' and Aalto's teaching methods can be derived from Goran Schildt's account of the views of the students at MIT. The 'realism' that Aalto offered was not a make-believe of office routine but a participation in the exploratory design process.

Finally, if we introduce into the equation the extent to which the identity and memorability of a building hinge upon the presence of metaphorical or symbolic analogies we find that, where the Harvard Centre seems aridly to repeat "a box is a box is a box", Baker House recalls in the monumental staircase the image of a great climbing vine while the sinuous curve of the south frontage recalls the undulation in the Charles River to the west before it runs past the building on its way to the sea.

Alvar and Aino Aalto
Baker House, MIT,
1947–1948.
Typical lounge and view
up the staircase.

CASE 4: THE HOUSE

It is important to the proper understanding of the Other Tradition that it should not be perceived in terms of any one formal language; this is particularly important since — as we have seen — the misleading labels 'Expressionist' and 'organic' have been applied to some of the work in this tradition. As a final case study therefore, I have chosen two houses, both of which set out to apply Le Corbusier's "Five Points of Architecture". What is revealed here, by the comparison, is the difference in application of those principles — one from the point of view of a Practical Art serving an end other than itself, the other from the point of a Fine Art as an end in itself. Eileen Gray's point of departure was the desire for a certain way of life — "the art of living" — and she saw the Five Points to be the best means by which she might satisfy that desire. Le Corbusier's point of departure was the wish to demonstrate the virtues of the Five Points (as exemplified by his Loucheur system) only to find that his application of them turned out to be undesirable as a way of life to his client.

The house that Le Corbusier designed and built for Mme de Mandrot, in 1929–1931, is a microcosm of his way of thinking and his relations with his clients: and as we shall see, it also has a hitherto unsuspected relationship to the house that Eileen Gray built at Roquebrune a few years later.

The client, Mme de Mandrot, was a close and influential friend of Le Corbusier. It will be remembered that it was she who had proposed and acted as hostess for the momentous first gathering of CIAM at La Sarraz in 1928. Le Corbusier wrote to her telling her that she had an important place in history: "It would seem that Madame de Mandrot, after the event of La Sarraz which gave her entry by the door of honour to the world of modern architecture, would be just right to live in a modern house."[5]

Le Corbusier
Maisons Loucheur,
1929.
Type plan.

In the autumn of 1929 she wrote to Le Corbusier asking him for a design: "not too expensive — something like your mother's house (four beds or so) and a garden"; and it was something like that house that she got in the end, but not until she had been led a dance through Le Corbusier's current preoccupation with something entirely different.

The house at Lake Leman for his mother (built in 1925) was a flat-roofed bungalow, linear in form, the main living area being in the centre with the visitor's bedroom at one end and the kitchen, bathroom and access to roof and cellar at the other. It was a house for two with no servants, covering an area of 50 metres — "*une véritable petite machine à habiter*". In essence, it was a load-bearing masonry construction open to the south along almost its entire length with an 11 metre long window facing the lake and the mountains beyond. The length of the whole house was 18 metres: the interior width, four metres. A walled garden embraced a patio with a smaller framed view of the lake.

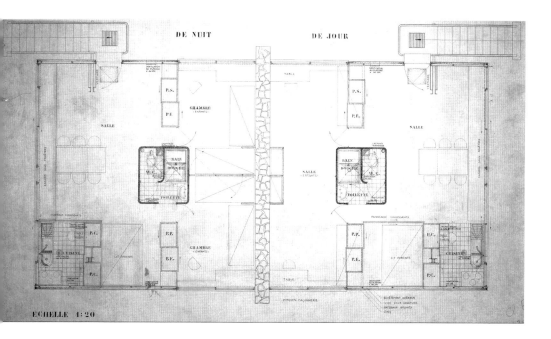

The most interesting fact about the nature of the initial design put forward for Mme de Mandrot was that it bore almost no relationship to the Lake Leman prototype. This is deeply revealing of Le Corbusier's approach to such a project. At the time of Mme de Mandrot's invitation, Le Corbusier was fully involved in developing the form of industrialised house-type commissioned by the Minister of Works, M Loucheur. This was based on a system of prefabricated frame construction with lightweight cladding panels in glass and zinc, and a core of plumbing assemblies for sanitary and kitchen services. It conformed to most of the

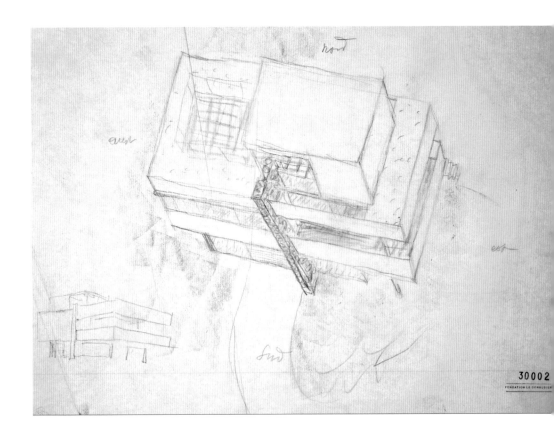

rules of the Five Points — *pilotis*, undercroft, roof garden, *fenêtres en longueur*. The elements could be combined in a number of different ways and we have already seen one such assembly in the dwelling unit proposed for the Ideal Farm. While the main elements were to be manufactured off-site, one concession was made to local traditional craft-building in the form of a 500 centimetre thick stone wall employed as either a party wall between two (semi-detached) dwellings or as a sound barrier between day and night use zones of a large house.

And so the first design offered to Mme de Mandrot took the form of a standard Loucheur double-unit house whose only feature shared with the Lake Leman prototype was the inclusion of a stone wall.

This apparently gratuitous offering illustrates an aspect of Le Corbusier's mind that was both its strength and its weakness: the attempt to raise every project to the level of a general issue of which it would then become a model demonstration. The intellectual force behind this aspiration is what gives all of his work a certain loftiness that, at the time, reinforced his role as both pacemaker and lawgiver.

Its inadequacy lay in the fact that it operated solely in the field of ideas which, furthermore, were ideas exclusively dedicated to the marriage of form and technology. Its role seems to have been concerned more with the justification of a system than with the quality of life in Le Pradet.

It is not necessary to pursue at length the shifts and changes in the development of this design, which have been recounted so ably by Tim Benton.[6] Suffice it to say that this initial scheme did not meet with the approval of Mme de Mandrot who pointed out her own discovery of local environmental factors such as fierce easterly winds and uncomfortable solar heat that were not addressed in that scheme.

Le Corbusier
Villa de Madame de
Mandrot, Le Pradet,
1929.

This first proposal was therefore abandoned — but not entirely. The wish to employ at least some elements of the Loucheur system persisted. And so the ghost of a four by four metre frame and panel system remained, although, as we shall see, not in the form originally intended.

At the next stage a very different prototype was adopted — the house that Le Corbusier had designed (but did not build) for M Errazuriz in Chile.[7] From then on it was broadly this family of forms that persisted: masonry walls enclosing the vestigial grid of a columnar sub-system reposing upon a built-up patio podium. The slope of the site allowed for a lower ground level garage and studio to underpin the bungalow superstructure. Tim Benton sums up his account of the tortuous development of this project as follows:

> The villa for Hélène de Mandrot is unusual in many respects in Le Corbusier's oeuvre. The range and disparity of the references are almost uniquely broad and contradictory. But in some ways the exception proves the rule. The progress of the design is embedded in the play of the ideal and the contingent, rebounding from one extreme to another, from the ultra-industrial to the Third World vernacular, from the site-independent to the 'paysagiste'.

Le Corbusier
Villa de Madame de Mandrot, Le Pradet, 1929.
North facade.

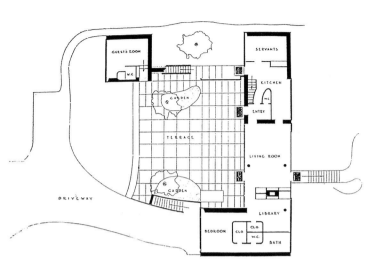

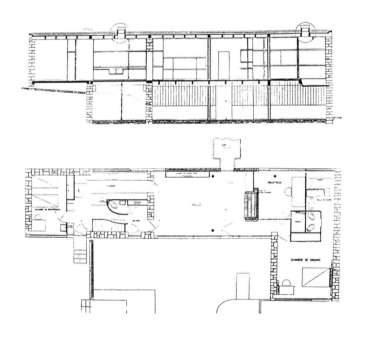

Le Corbusier
Villa de Madame de
Mandrot, Le Pradet,
1929.
Upper level plan,
long section
and lower level plan.

Let us examine the final design. Le Corbusier's own description of the house is brief:

> The composition takes its order from the landscape. The house occupies a little promontory overlooking the plain behind Toulon with its backdrop of mountains with a magnificent silhouette. We have tried to preserve the sensation of surprise that is offered by the unexpected vista of this immense landscape: and for that reason we have walled in the rooms on the side facing the view and then simply pierced it with a doorway which, when it is thrown open, reveals a platform from which the whole spectacle bursts into view like an explosion. Descending a narrow stair into the garden you will then see a large sculpture by Lipchitz on a stele whose top cuts into the sky above the mountains.
>
> On the opposite (south) side the more enclosed view is used to give life to the interior of the rooms and in the foreground has a raised garden which acts as the main base and connects the main body of the house to the freestanding pavilion which is for visiting friends.[8]

Le Corbusier
Villa de Madame de
Mandrot, Le Pradet,
1929.
Views of the south
facade.

The strength of this building lies in certain aspects that stem from a vision of the building viewed as an object. There is a certain drama in the projection of a platform and stairway to the garden springing from the sheer north face of the house: a sensual liveliness in the play between mass and frame, and an immediate satisfaction in the proportional coherence. There is wit in the weaving pattern of movement through the building that produces a *promenade architecturale* to the 'surprise' view of the north. So far so good. But where do you ever come to rest? The space of the living room is not large; it has two (structurally unnecessary) columns in it as a last vestige of the Loucheur system (albeit they are no longer lightweight metal elements but reinforced concrete); and, though small, the room is attacked by four doors and a corridor. Furthermore, the two external doors are in line, thus cutting a passage across the face of the fireplace (what about those fierce winds?). There is a strange set of wraparound perspective drawings, clearly not in Le Corbusier's hand (perhaps that of Maekawa Kunio, who was working as an assistant in his office at the time) which explore the surrounding surfaces but convey nothing at all of the spatial reality within. Where do you sit in relation to light and view? Where do you eat?

Le Corbusier
Villa de Madame de
Mandrot, Le Pradet,
1929.
Interiors.

And then other doubts crowd in. Is not the handling of the one marvellous view to the north a trifle too theatrical? When all the talk is done you have to work hard to enjoy it, and you do so by going out onto a platform that is too small to sit on. And surprise, after all, only comes once. To the south, where the Loucheur lightweight panel system survived in principle, one of the three viewing panes and all the upper panes were subsequently filled in with wooden panels to reduce the solar gain.

It is as if every design proposal, ingenious in itself, was made without thought of its interaction, so that in the event each had the unhappy effect of negating the other. Le Corbusier seems to have made no attempt to project himself into an existential appreciation of the whole living context; and one is uncomfortably reminded of the comment in the days of the Unité d'Habitation in Marseille that "this man has never changed a nappy in his life".

The house was finished in July 1931. By December, Mme de Mandrot wrote to Le Corbusier to say that she had left the house ("... absolutely uninhabitable"). The reasons she gave were to do with leaks (water and

wind) through the roof and both the solid and curtain wall. But the more you study that living room, the more you come to believe that it is the architecture of the room that is simply uninhabitable. At the end of the affair Le Corbusier concluded the letter in which he had said that Mme de Mandrot ought to have been "just right to live in a modern house", with the words, "you have shown us that the answer is no. *Que diable alors!*" Could it not be that after all it was not Mme de Mandrot who failed to be "just right to live in a modern house", but that the house was just not right to live in?

This, however, did not prevent Le Corbusier from proclaiming that:

> the house is one of our best.... In spite of the employment of ordinary stone masonry, the theses that we always exploit in our houses come together again here. The classification is made very clear between the load bearing walls and the glazed panels which enclose the empty spaces...!!

Le Corbusier
Villa de Madame de
Mandrot, Le Pradet,
1929.
North facade.

Between 1926–1929 Eileen Gray designed and built a house at Cap Martin Roquebrune for Jean Badovici and herself. It was named E1027 and Badovici, who was editor of the periodical *L'Architecture Vivante*, dedicated a whole number to the house entitled "Maison en bord de Mer", with many drawings, 63 photographs and various texts which included a dialogue between himself and Eileen Gray.[9]

The text was described at the time as "disquieting".[10] It was certainly one of the very first to challenge the early spread of formalism and deserves a place of honour in any records of the Resistance; furthermore, a number of Eileen Gray's targets were quite explicitly formulated in Corbusian language. As we have seen, her point of view and language are very close to Aalto and Haering. The dwelling was 'a living organism' in which "each of the inhabitants could, if need be, find total independence and an atmosphere of solitude and concentration. Nowhere has one sought a form for its own sake: everywhere one has thought of people, of their sensibilities and of what they need", and again, "art is founded on a habit, but not on the artificial habit that creates fashion. What is necessary is to give to the object the form best suited to the spontaneous gesture or instinctive reflex which corresponds to its use."

Eileen Gray
E1027: House at Roquebrune, 1926–1929. Upper level plan and lower level plan.

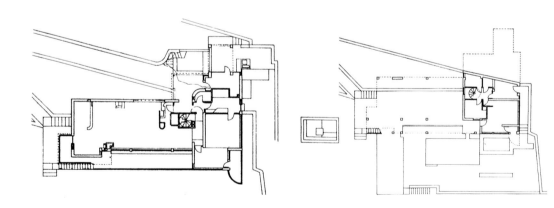

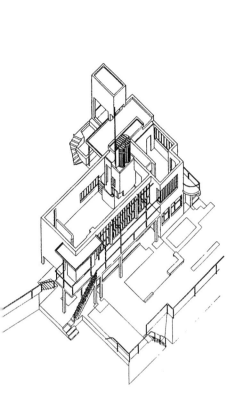

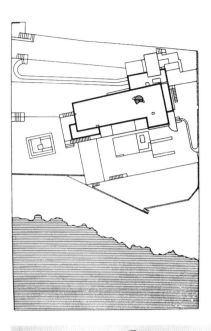

<u>CLOCKWISE</u>
<u>FROM ABOVE</u>:
Eileen Gray
E1027: House at
Roquebrune, 1926–1929.
Axonometric.
Site plan.
View from the south.

Quite clearly the point of origin of her work lies in the pursuit of what she called "the art of living", rather than the art of architecture — Gray had a unique gift for turning the practical into the poetic.

The first impression that one gets of the house itself is of an ocean vessel perched halfway up the rocky escarpment from sea level, as if it had been stranded there on a freak high-tide. Closer inspection shows that it is very delicately locked into the ledge-like contours of the rock face, grounded only at the entrance and kitchen patio but for the rest, scrupulously obeying the rules of the "Five Points of Architecture" — *pilotis*, garden beneath, roof-terrace above, *fenêtres en longueur*, free plan. The whole composition has an incomparable precision and vitality, and the air of a vessel launched in the springtime for a "*Voyage à Cythère*" — to borrow a metaphor from Gray's own wall piece, "*Invitation au Voyage*":

> The house is built for a man who likes work, sport and to entertain friends. Although it is very small it must be arranged in a way that allows the occupier to receive friends and put them completely at ease. In this small house we have tried to give expression equally to two different ways of life: the idea of 'camping' which responds to the need for casual outwardness and the normal idea which tries to give to the individual an independent and private place where one can develop one's own deeper powers.
>
> The entrance is played down as suits a place where windows and doors are rarely closed: but on the other hand one has sought an architectural layout which screens the interior from the exterior and does not make a door that one fears can burst open at any moment or perhaps invite an unwelcome visit. The same arrangement has been adopted for the individual rooms. The place of arrival is a big covered space, a sort of atrium, large, welcoming and not like those narrow little doors which seem to open only grudgingly. Straight ahead a large bare wall, suggesting a sort of resistance plain and clear cut; the door to the right leads into the main house, the door to the left into the service area. By the right hand door a folding screen prevents a view into the room from the outside when the door is opened.[11]

<u>TOP TO BOTTOM:</u>
Eileen Gray
E1027: House at
Roquebrune, 1926–1929.
Garden front,
entrance patio and
entrance approach.

Eileen Gray
E 1027: House at
Roquebrune, 1926–1929.
Living room (top) and
bedroom/study.

The large (14 x 6.5 metre) living room, while facing the sun from morning to evening, monitors the level of light and ventilation by a layering of elements that Gray likened to the shutter of a camera. No other designer has ever equalled the range and finesse of technical invention and wit deployed here, covering the whole range of architecture, fittings, furniture and fabrics all of a piece.

Her moulding of space was just as precisely tuned. In order to accord to every spatial episode the integrity and independence that it needed, she "took the axis of entrance off the wall to avoid the doors being visible" (remember the living room at Le Pradet that was directly under attack from four doors and two corridors):

> Architecture of the exterior seems to have interested architects of the avant-garde at the expense of architecture of the interior. As if a house were to be conceived for the pleasure of the eye rather than for the wellbeing of the inhabitants.... The interior plan should not be the accidental consequence of the facade: it should enjoy a complete life, logical and harmonious. Far from being subordinate to the modelling of the exterior it should, on the contrary, determine it.

Eileen Gray
E 1027: House at
Roquebrune, 1926–1929.
Living room and mirror.

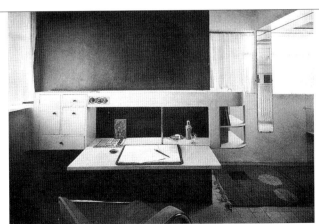
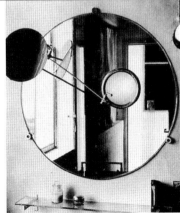

Peter Adam quotes a number of passages from Gray's notebooks which exemplify very poetically the frame of mind which I have described earlier as perceptions of habitability: "The desire to penetrate... a transition which still keeps the mystery of the object one is going to see, which keeps the pleasure in suspense." "Movement in building should follow the walls in such a natural way that the pictorial objects inside reveal themselves gradually to the spectator." "Entering a house is like the sensation of entering a mouth which will close behind you... or like the sensation of pleasure when one arrives with a boat in a harbour, the feeling of being enclosed but free to circulate."

When Gray wrote that "a window without a shutter is like an eye without an eyelid", she offered an insight into the nature of much of her work — whether furniture or architecture. It is that they contained a component (often mobile) which acted upon its environment — filtering, screening, shading, reflecting, extending. And this interactive response of the parts reinforced the sense of a living presence to the whole, a faculty of animation that far exceeds the simple *convenance* of rational layout. There is a passage in Rilke's description of the reciprocity of part to part in a painting by Cézanne which attests to the same quality: "It's as if every place were aware of all the other places."[12] Such animation shows also the capability of the space there to change in response to occasion or the time of day or season's weather. She continues:

> When the sea is rough and the horizon gloomy, one has only to close the large bay window to the south, draw the curtain, and then open the small bay window to the north, which gives on to a garden of lemon trees and the old village, to find a new horizon where masses of greenery replace the broad expanses of blue and grey.

Eileen Gray
E 1027: House at
Roquebrune, 1926–1929.
Guest bedroom.

By the same token, it is significant that rather than the Corbusian concept of '*promenade*', Gray uses the analogy with choreography which engages simultaneously all quarters of a space in mutual interaction.

Her approach evolves from the experiences of inhabiting a particular house in a particular place. Her values, however sophisticated in application, have, paradoxically, the intimacy, responsiveness and authenticity that we normally consider to be unique to those structures that we call 'primitive' — that is to say, carried out by the inhabitants themselves, using only their own hands and the materials locally to hand, coping with the prevailing environment, developing any and every advantage from local topography, and erecting means of defence against any adverse conditions. Because whatever disadvantages accrue from the limitations of this primitive mode, they are vastly outweighed by the enormous advantage that is gained by virtue of the inhabitant being the agent. Not only are the original decisions generated by some vision of a desired way of life, but a continuous process of feedback from all members of the family will ensue so that modification, extension or reduction can be met with an equally immediate response. The dwelling that has been made by the hands of its inhabitants can as easily be reshaped. In Gray's case the means are, of course, very sophisticated as well as very direct.

Prunella Clough has described a "rather absurd" episode during a visit to the 1958 Brussels Exhibition, in which Eileen Gray suddenly stopped in her tracks, as if thunderstruck, by the sight of a certain rubber floormat. She would not move. She was caught up in an intense meditation on how that material could be used. We read of similar insights experienced by Sigurd Lewerentz and it is perhaps not surprising that these two artists who used their medium with such intensity and purity, who said everything that they had to say by a certain way of building, should see, in a chance encounter with a new piece of material, a whole range of unprecedented possibilities open up, as Mozart might, from an initial phrase, suddenly perceive a whole symphony fall into place in his mind. On the other hand, Gray quite explicitly says that "the thing made is more important than the way it was made which must always be of secondary importance".

Eileen Gray
E1027: House at
Roquebrune, 1926–1929.
Wardrobe.

Le Corbusier painting
a mural in E1027,
Roquebrune, 1926–1929.

Eileen Gray's commanding technical skill was grounded on her earlier pieces of furniture, her insistence upon practising the craft herself and her eagerness to assimilate the newly available materials. It was in the first instance brought to bear upon precisely that mediating world between furniture and architecture, environment and structure, whose medium of communication is the sensibility towards body-language that we have described in terms of habitability.

Throughout this description, which significantly gains greatly from the use of her own terminology, we are led to an application of the Five Points and their extension into finer and finer detail which has the internal continuity of serving a deeply studied and fully realised end.

NOTES—CHAPTER FIVE

1   Haering, Hugo, *Strukturprobleme des bauens*.
2   Rudolph, Paul, *Perspecta*, no. 7, p. 41.
3   Herdeg, Klaus, *The Decorated Diagram*, Cambridge, MA: MIT Press, 1983.
4   Poodry, Deborah and Victoria Ozonoff, "Coffins, Pies & Couches: Aalto at MIT", *Space & Society*, MIT Group ed., no. 18, June 1982.
5   Benton, Tim, "The Villa de Mandrot and the Place of Imagination", *Quaderns*, October 1984.
6   Benton, "The Villa de Mandrot and the Place of Imagination".
7   Le Corbusier and Pierre Jeanneret, *Oeuvre Complète*, les Editions d'Architecture, vol. 2, 1929–1934, Zurich: Erlenbach, 1947, pp. 48–52.
8   Le Corbusier and Jeanneret, *Oeuvre Complète*, pp. 58–62.
9   Badovici, Jean, *L'Architecture Vivante*, 1923–1933, 22 vols, Paris: Automne & Hiver, 1929. One cannot discuss this house without reference to Le Corbusier's own obsession with it. In the first place he persuaded Badovici in 1939 to let him paint a number of murals in it in spite of Eileen Gray's own claim that, apart from her 'Invitation' there was deliberately no place for paintings on the walls. She understandably found the murals distasteful both in principle and in their handling, and never visited the house again. Le Corbusier built his work, Cabanon, alongside the house and when Badovici died, went to extreme lengths to persuade one of his friends to buy the house which he loved and in which he was living at the time of his death.
10 Adam, Peter, *Eileen Gray: Architect Designer*, London: Thames and Hudson, 1987.
11 Quotations from Eileen Gray are, unless otherwise stated, from the description of the house in "From Eclecticism to Doubt", dialogue Eileen Gray/Jean Badovici in *L'Architecture Vivante*.
12 Rilke, RM, *Letters on Cézanne*, London: Jonathan Cape, 1988.

POSTSCRIPT

It is not what a building looks like on the day it is opened but what it is like thirty years later that matters.

ALVAR AALTO

The line of argument followed in this book could equally have been pursued in reverse order. We have proceeded from the recognition of a polemical moment in history at 'the birth of the Modern Movement'; moved to a discussion of the rival doctrine that it provoked; entered a claim for a certain interpretation of the ensuing events; and concluded by a presentation of the evidence in exemplary case studies for defence or prosecution in the light of that claim. But one might have proceeded in the opposite sequence by starting from the demonstrable success of a particular building and then trying to deduce the reasons for that success. Indeed, in the Prologue I made the point that this was the way in which the theme first emerged out of my *Architectural Reflections*, which originated in an interest in ostensibly quite unrelated phenomena.[1]

To anyone who has been sufficiently persuaded by the thesis of this book, I would like to propose that they too pursue the latter course; and by selecting a building that has prospered in use over a number of years and still has the power to excite the mind and touch the heart, they should proceed to analyse it back to the source of its origin and inspiration in idea. I have produced an argument that I believe entails pragmatic consequences of substance — but it is up to the reader to put it to the test.

It is an inevitable consequence of my claim for the existence of an Other Tradition of Modern Architecture that one has to ask whether that Tradition has a future. In the historical context, I believe that what I have demonstrated is not only a true analysis of 'what went wrong' but also offers a critical basis upon which correct action might be grounded. I have necessarily taken examples and references from at least thirty years ago because verification in use (Aalto's 30-year rule) is the one criterion by which my thesis should be validated. This does not mean that I fail to believe that, in the intervening years, there has been much work that will eventually be validated in the same way. One could, for example, point to the exemplary work over the last 30 years and more in Urbino by Giancarlo de Carlo, in which new buildings and adaptation of old buildings have the quality of variety, invention and conviction that have served a wide variety of ends for the city to the obvious satisfaction of the community.[2] And it is my firm belief that in the future, a comparison between the British Library and the Très Grande Bibliothèque will prove to be a firm corroboration of my argument!

What I hope I have shown is that, ever since the betrayal of the initial intentions of the Modern Movement, criticism, action and reaction have almost inevitably reeled from wrong to wrong. Many of the causes for concern within the discipline itself were reflected in factors operating in fields outside the discipline — sociological and economic. This is not something to be surprised at or to recoil from in distaste; on the contrary, it is of the essence that these concerns took the form of a need other than that of the discipline of architecture itself. It was precisely their task to do so. Where architecture was truly employed to serve such a cause, it was triumphant both as architecture and as a service to its society — inseparably so. Where it was deflected from its goal, it failed — in both. One of the ways in which such failures have been denigrated is to sneer at the 'good intentions' and withdraw into the shell of an increasingly solipsistic concern with the discipline *in vacua*.

This was already apparent in the interpretations of Le Corbusier's late work, where his extraordinary range of interests was reflected, however obscurely, in his *Poème de L'Angle Droit* and illustrations of the *Iliad*. But it was with the protagonists of 'Postmodernism' that this trend revealed its fundamental contradictions and triviality, withdrawing further into exercises called 'cardboard architecture' or 'autonomous architecture' or into the past for the comfortable joys of 're-enchantment'. One would only have to take as a case study the three alternative designs (one of them by Philip Johnson) for the London Bridge Development to recognise a return to the 'Battle of the Styles' in a way that needs no gloss from me.

Conversely, as we have seen, the work in the springtime of the movement before 1928, particularly in Holland and Germany, demonstrated a variety of freshness and sanity that could inspire the poet Auden to speak of "a change of heart" and still today remains a bracing challenge.

This huge achievement is not to be shrugged off patronisingly as "the architecture of good intentions". Within that spectrum of need, the intentions were classically correct; the architecture very good.

I have tried to account for 'what went wrong' within the mainstream of the architectural discipline itself, but of course there were even more powerful forces outside the discipline itself — economic, demographic and political that, in the words of Habermas, "are not primarily problems of design but

Giancarlo de Carlo
The Magistero, Urbino,
1968–1976.

rather problems of controlling and managing anonymous systems that invade urban life and threaten to consume its fabric".[3] The widespread adoption of 'building-systems' blatantly based upon financial economy in the mass-production of construction components, and quite lacking in any commitment whatsoever to adequate management and maintenance, has brought blanket discredit upon a venture that was an enormous success in its salad days. This is one example among many in which some of the early pre-CIAM work of the 'Resistance' has been damned by being identified with its usurper. One of the difficulties at this time in representing such work is precisely the task of disengagement from its travesty, the current denigration employed by the Postmodern 'avant-garde of the Great Retreat'. For it also needs to be repeated that the charge that the 'Postmodernists' have brought against Gropius' rejection of historical reference is quite irrelevant to the work of architects like Asplund and Aalto. We have already made the point that one has only to look at Asplund's varied solutions for the Lawcourts building in Gothenburg, the inexhaustible richness of Aalto's Villa Mairea in which Purist abstractions are woven through with themes from Karelian vernacular and the two figures interlocked so that past and present shake hands to see that this work was in no need of stylistic 're-enchantment'.

When, 50 years ago, Aalto wrote "it is not the rationalization that was wrong in the first (and now past) period of modern architecture: the wrongness lies in the fact that the rationalization has not gone deep enough", he could have been speaking for all of the architects whom, in his Discourse at the RIBA he had called the "Garde d'honneur of the hard-fighting squadron" and whose work and theory I have tried to rehearse.[4]

It is that work alone that offers a constructive model for what Jurgen Habermas has boldly saluted as 'the uncompleted project'.

NOTES—POSTSCRIPT

1   Colin St John, Wilson, *Architectural Reflections*, Oxford: Butterworth Heinneman, 1992, reprint 1994.
2   Colin St John Wilson on Giancarlo de Carlo, "Master of the Resistance", *Architectural Review*, July 1993.
3   Habermas, Jürgen, "Post Modern Architecture", Munich Conference, 1981.
4   Aalto, Alvar, "Art and Technology", 1955, in *Sketches*, Cambridge, MA: MIT Press, 1978.

INDEX

PICTURE CREDITS

Unless otherwise indicated, all visual material in *The Other Tradition of Modern Architecture The Uncompleted Project* is courtesy of Colin St John Wilson and was previously published in the 1995 Academy Group edition of this work.

Written by Colin St John Wilson

Designed by Rachel Pfleger © bdp

Black Dog Publishing Limited
Unit 4.4 Tea Building
56 Shoreditch High Street
London
E1 6JJ

Tel: +44 (0)20 7613 1922
Fax: +44 (0)20 7613 1944
Email: info@bdp.demon.co.uk

All opinions expressed within this publication are those of the author and not necessarily of the publisher.

British Library Cataloguing-in-Publication Data.
A CIP record for this book is available from the British Library.

ISBN10 1 904772 62 5
ISBN13 978 1 904772 62 0

architecture art design
fashion history photography
theory and things

www.bdpworld.com

Black Dog Publishing is an environmentally responsible company. *The Other Tradition of Modern Architecture The Uncompleted Project* is printed on Evolution Satin a 70% FSC recycled fibre and 30% FSC certified virgin fibre chlorine free paper.